Kaplan Publishing are constantly finding new ways to make a difference to your studies and our exciting online resources really do offer something different to students looking for exam success.

This book comes with free MyKaplan online resources so that you can study anytime, anywhere. **This free online resource is not sold separately and is included in the price of the book.**

Having purchased this book, you have access to the following online study materials:

CONTENT	AAT	
	Text	Kit
Electronic version of the book	✓	✓
Progress tests with instant answers	✓	
Mock assessments online	✓	✓
Material updates	✓	✓

How to access your online resources

Kaplan Financial students will already have a MyKaplan account and these extra resources will be available to you online. You do not need to register again, as this process was completed when you enrolled. If you are having problems accessing online materials, please ask your course administrator.

If you are not studying with Kaplan and did not purchase your book via a Kaplan website, to unlock your extra online resources please go to www.mykaplan.co.uk/addabook (even if you have set up an account and registered books previously). You will then need to enter the ISBN number (on the title page and back cover) and the unique pass key number contained in the scratch panel below to gain access. You will also be required to enter additional information during this process to set up or confirm your account details.

If you purchased through Kaplan Flexible Learning or via the Kaplan Publishing website you will automatically receive an e-mail invitation to MyKaplan. Please register your details using this email to gain access to your content. If you do not receive the e-mail or book content, please contact Kaplan Publishing.

Your Code and Information

This code can only be used once for the registration of one book online. This registration and your online content will expire when the final sittings for the examinations covered by this book have taken place. Please allow one hour from the time you submit your book details for us to process your request.

D0258670

Please scratch the film to access your MyKaplan code.

Please be aware that this code is case-sensitive and you will need to include the dashes within the passcode, but not when entering the ISBN. For further technical support, please visit www.MyKaplan.co.uk

KAPLAN

PUBLISHING

AQ2016

Using Accounting Software

EXAM KIT

This Exam Kit supports study for the following AAT qualifications:

AAT Foundation Certificate in Accounting – Level 2

AAT Foundation Diploma in Accounting and Business – Level 2

AAT Foundation Certificate in Bookkeeping – Level 2

AAT Foundation Award in Accounting Software – Level 2

AAT Level 2 Award in Accounting Skills to Run Your Business

AAT Foundation Certificate in Accounting at SCQF Level 5

KAPLAN

PUBLISHING

British Library Cataloguing-in-Publication Data

A catalogue record for this book is available from the British Library.

Published by:

Kaplan Publishing UK

Unit 2 The Business Centre

Molly Millar's Lane

Wokingham

Berkshire

RG41 2QZ

ISBN: 978-1-78740-526-4

© Kaplan Financial Limited, 2019

Printed and bound in Great Britain.

CONTENTS

Features in this exam kit

In addition to providing a wide ranging bank of real exam style questions, we have also included in this kit:

- Paper specific information and advice on exam technique.

- Our recommended approach to make your revision for this particular subject as effective as possible.

You will find a wealth of other resources to help you with your studies on MyKaplan and AAT websites:

www.mykaplan.co.uk

www.aat.org.uk/

Quality and accuracy are of the utmost importance to us so if you spot an error in any of our products, please send an email to mykaplanreporting@kaplan.com with full details, or follow the link to the feedback form in MyKaplan.

Our Quality Co-ordinator will work with our technical team to verify the error and take action to ensure it is corrected in future editions.

UNIT-SPECIFIC INFORMATION

THE EXAM

FORMAT OF THE ASSESSMENT

The assessment will consist of one part and will cover the learning outcomes listed in the table below.

In any one assessment, students may not be assessed on all content, or on the full depth or breadth of a piece of content. The content assessed may change over time to ensure validity of assessment, but all assessment criteria will be tested over time.

The learning outcomes for this unit are as follows:

	Learning outcome	Weighting
1	Set up accounting software	25%
2	Process sales and purchases transactions	35%
3	Process bank and cash transactions	20%
4	Perform period end routine tasks	15%
5	Produce reports	5%
	Total	100%

Time allowed

2 hours

PASS MARK

The pass mark for all AAT CBAs is 70%.

Always keep your eye on the clock and make sure you attempt all questions!

DETAILED SYLLABUS

The detailed syllabus and study guide written by the AAT can be found at:

www.aat.org.uk/

INDEX TO PRACTICE QUESTIONS

EXAM TECHNIQUE

- **Do not skip any of the material** in the syllabus.

- **Read each question** *very* carefully.

- **Double-check your answer** before committing yourself to it.

- Answer **every** question – if you do not know an answer to a multiple choice question or true/false question, you don't lose anything by guessing. Think carefully before you **guess**.

- If you are answering a multiple-choice question, **eliminate first those answers that you know are wrong**. Then choose the most appropriate answer from those that are left.

- **Don't panic** if you realise you've answered a question incorrectly. Getting one question wrong will not mean the difference between passing and failing

Computer-based exams – tips

- Do not attempt a CBA until you have **completed all study material** relating to it.

- On the AAT website there is a CBA demonstration. It is **ESSENTIAL** that you attempt this before your real CBA. You will become familiar with how to move around the CBA screens and the way that questions are formatted, increasing your confidence and speed in the actual exam.

- Be sure you understand how to use the **software** before you start the exam. If in doubt, ask the assessment centre staff to explain it to you.

- Questions are **displayed on the screen** and answers are entered using keyboard and mouse. At the end of the exam, you are given a certificate showing the result you have achieved.

- In addition to the traditional multiple-choice question type, CBAs will also contain **other types of questions**, such as number entry questions, drag and drop, true/false, pick lists or drop down menus or hybrids of these.

- In some CBAs you will have to type in complete computations or written answers.

- You need to be sure you **know how to answer questions** of this type before you sit the exam, through practice.

KAPLAN'S RECOMMENDED REVISION APPROACH

QUESTION PRACTICE IS THE KEY TO SUCCESS

Success in professional examinations relies upon you acquiring a firm grasp of the required knowledge at the tuition phase. In order to be able to do the questions, knowledge is essential.

However, the difference between success and failure often hinges on your exam technique on the day and making the most of the revision phase of your studies.

The **Kaplan Study Text** is the starting point, designed to provide the underpinning knowledge to tackle all questions. However, in the revision phase, poring over text books is not the answer.

Kaplan Pocket Notes are designed to help you quickly revise a topic area; however you then need to practise questions. There is a need to progress to exam style questions as soon as possible, and to tie your exam technique and technical knowledge together.

The importance of question practice cannot be over-emphasised.

The recommended approach below is designed by expert tutors in the field, in conjunction with their knowledge of the examiner and the specimen assessment.

You need to practise as many questions as possible in the time you have left.

OUR AIM

Our aim is to get you to the stage where you can attempt exam questions confidently, to time, in a closed book environment, with no supplementary help (i.e. to simulate the real examination experience).

Practising your exam technique is also vitally important for you to assess your progress and identify areas of weakness that may need more attention in the final run up to the examination.

In order to achieve this we recognise that initially you may feel the need to practice some questions with open book help.

Good exam technique is vital.

THE KAPLAN UACS REVISION PLAN

Stage 1: Assess areas of strengths and weaknesses

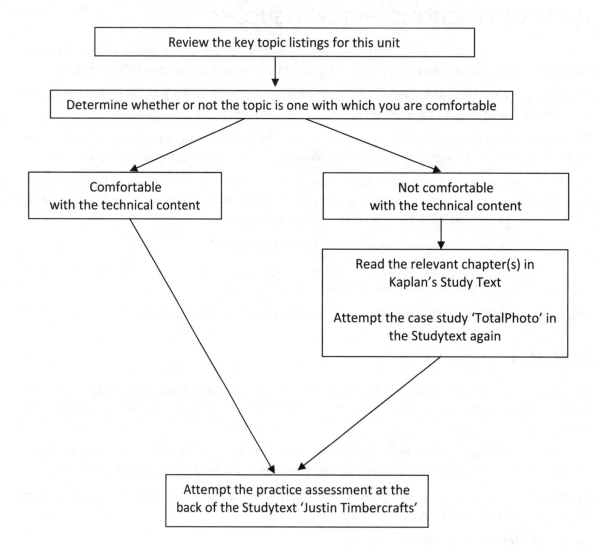

Stage 2: Practice scenarios

Follow the order of practice scenarios as presented in this Kit and attempt the questions in the order suggested.

Try to avoid referring to Study Texts and your notes and the model answer until you have completed your attempt.

Review your attempt with the model answer and assess how much of the answer you achieved.

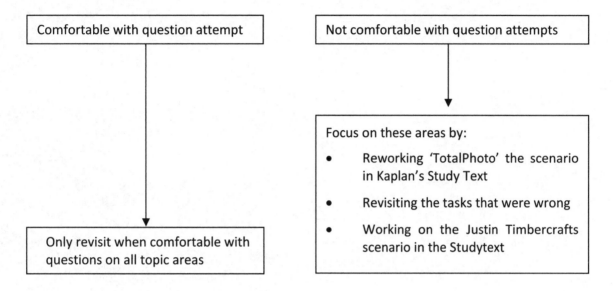

Comfortable with question attempt	Not comfortable with question attempts

Only revisit when comfortable with questions on all topic areas

Focus on these areas by:

- Reworking 'TotalPhoto' the scenario in Kaplan's Study Text
- Revisiting the tasks that were wrong
- Working on the Justin Timbercrafts scenario in the Studytext

Stage 3: Final pre-exam revision

We recommend that you **attempt at least one two hour mock examination** containing a set of previously unseen exam standard questions.

Attempt the mock CBA online in timed, closed book conditions to simulate the real exam experience.

KAPLAN PUBLISHING

Section 1

PRACTICE QUESTIONS

PRACTICE PAPER 1

TOY SHOP

THE SITUATION

This assignment is based on an existing business, Toy Shop, a small manufacturer who has recently set up in business selling:

- Boxed Games
- Computer games
- Jigsaws

The owner of the business is James Free who operates as a sole trader.

At the start of the business James operated a manual bookkeeping system but has now decided that from 1st May 20XX the accounting system will become computerised.

You can assume that all documentation has been checked and authorised by James Free.

Some nominal ledger accounts have already been allocated suitable account codes. **You may need to amend or create other account codes.**

Set the company's Financial Year to start in May of the current year.

Their company details are:-

Toy Shop

64 Long Lane

Langhorne

North Yorkshire

YO21 3EJ

Tel: 01234 567891

You are employed as an accounting technician.

The business is registered for VAT. The rate of VAT charged on all goods and services sold by Toy Shops is 20%. VAT registration number 123456789.

TASK 1

Refer to the customer listing below and set up customer records to open Sales Ledger accounts for each customer.

Customer account code	Customer name, address and contact details	Customer account details
BB01	Busy Bee Toys 832 High Street Oxford OX2 3WG	Credit limit: £4000 Payment Terms: 30 days Opening Balance: £349.20 (relates to invoice 021 dated 12th Apr)
FF02	Forming Fun 21 Newton Quay Knott Mill Manchester M6 3RJ	Credit limit: £4000 Payment Terms: 30 days Opening Balance: £99.60 (relates to invoice 035 dated 8th Apr)
SM03	Space Models 13 Central Street Perth Scotland SC4 8RQ	Credit limit: £3000 Payment Terms: 30 days Opening Balance: £1195.20 (relates to invoice 093 dated 10th Apr)
TP04	Teddy T's Party 3 Paradise Street Wokingham WO4 6QP	Credit limit: £7000 Payment Terms: 30 days Opening Balance: £579.60 (relates to invoice 1003 dated 17th Apr)

TASK 2

Refer to the supplier listing below and set up supplier records to open Purchase Ledger accounts for each supplier.

Supplier account code	Supplier name, address and contact details	Supplier account details
PL01	Abacus C & C Unit 31 Kitts Industrial Estate St Helens Lancs	Credit limit: £5500 Payment Terms: 30 days Opening Balance: £369.60 (relates to invoice B/1874 dated 2nd Apr)
PL02	Compugames Ltd 6 Jury Road Dublin Eire	Credit limit: £4000 Payment Terms: 30 days Opening Balance: £511.20 (relates to invoice 1087 dated 11th Apr)
PL03	Space Models 13 Central Street Perth Scotland	Credit limit: £2000 Payment Terms: 30 days Opening Balance: £306 (relates to invoice F-0193 dated 18th Apr)
PL04	Toys Unlimited 95 Cuscaden Road Edinburgh Scotland	Credit limit: £2000 Payment Terms: 30 days Opening Balance: £970.80 (relates to invoice W/032 dated 18th Apr)

TASK 3.1

Refer to the list of General ledger balances below. Enter the opening balances onto the computerised accounting system, making sure you select/create/amend the appropriate general ledger account codes.

List of general ledger balances as at the **1st May**

Account name	DR	CR
	£	£
Furniture and fixtures	5800.00	
Motor Vehicles	3000.00	
Bank	4225.00	
Petty Cash	300.00	
Sales Ledger Control Account *	2223.60	
Purchase Ledger Control Account *		2157.60
VAT on sales		543.00
VAT on purchases	109.00	
Capital		20000.00
Drawings	355.00	
Sales – Computer Games		6080.00
Sales – Jigsaws		700.00
Sales – Boxed Games		1967.00
Purchases – Computer Games	8000.00	
Purchases – Jigsaws	3200.00	
Purchases – Boxed Games	2465.00	
Office Stationery	53.00	
Electricity	167.00	
Rent and Rates	1550.00	
Note You do not need to enter these figures as you have already entered opening balances for customers and suppliers		

TASK 3.2

Transfer £500 from the bank current account to the bank deposit account. Enter this on the computerised accounting system using reference TRANS01 dated 1st May.

TASK 3.3

Produce the following reports and **identify and correct any errors**:

- Customer Address List
- Supplier Address List
- Trial Balance Report

TASK 4

Enter the following sales invoices and credit note onto the computerised accounting system.

Toy Shops
64 Long Lane
Langhorne
North Yorkshire
YO21 3EJ

Telephone: 0121 765 3213
Email: jp@toyshops.co.uk

Sales Invoice No 2021

Date: 4th May 20XX

Busy Bee Toys
832 High Street
Oxford
OX2 3WG

Description	£
Computer Games	2585.00
VAT @ 20.00%	517.00
Total for payment	3102.00

Terms 30 days

Toy Shops
64 Long Lane
Langhorne
North Yorkshire
YO21 3EJ

Telephone: 0121 765 3213
Email: jp@toyshops.co.uk

Sales Invoice No 2022

Date: 4th May 20XX

Forming Fun
21 Newton Quay
Knott Mill
Manchester
M6 3RJ

Description	£
Boxed Games	500.00
VAT @ 20.00%	100.00
Total for payment	600.00

Terms 30 days

KAPLAN PUBLISHING

Toy Shops
64 Long Lane
Langhorne
North Yorkshire
YO21 3EJ

Telephone: 0121 765 3213
Email: jp@toyshops.co.uk

Sales Invoice No 2023

Date: 6th May 20XX

Teddy T's Party
3 Paradise Street
Wokingham
WO4 6QP

Description	£
Computer games	5000.00
VAT @ 20.00%	1000.00
Total for payment	6000.00

Terms 30 days

Toy Shops
64 Long Lane
Langhorne
North Yorkshire
YO21 3EJ

Telephone: 0121 765 3213
Email: jp@toyshops.co.uk

Credit Note No CN101

Date: 13th May 20XX

Teddy T's Party
3 Paradise Street
Wokingham
WO4 6QP

Description	£
Return faulty Computer games	320.00
VAT @ 20.00%	64.00
Total credit	384.00

TASK 5.1

Enter the following purchases invoices onto the computer system.

Date	A/C No.	Invoice Ref	Gross	Vat	Net	Computer games	Jigsaws	Boxed Games
3rd May	PL01	B/989	540.00	90.00	450.00	450.00		
5th May	PL02	145215	600.00	100.00	500.00			500.00
10th May	PL03	C-32632	1200.00	200.00	1000.00	1000.00		
10th May	PL04	12421	18.00	0.00	18.00		18.00	

TASK 5.2

Enter the following purchase credit note onto the computer system.

Date	Supplier	N/C	Credit Note Ref	Description	Details
15th May	Compugames	5000	11245	Computer Games	£88.00 Plus tax

TASK 6

The following remittance advices were received from customers. Enter the receipts onto the computerised accounting system.

Busy Bee Toys
Remittance Advice
To: Toy Shop Date: 17 May 20XX   A cheque for £349.20 (number 100322) is attached in payment of invoice no 021.

Forming Fun
Remittance Advice
To: Toy Shop Date: 17 May 20XX   A cheque for £99.60 (number 267543) is attached in payment of invoice 035.

Teddy T's Party	
BACS Remittance Advice	

To: Toy Shop

Date: 26 May 20XX

An amount of £195.60 has been paid directly into your bank account in payment of invoice 1003, including credit note CN101.

TASK 7

The following cheque payments were sent to suppliers; enter the payments on the accounts system. **Produce the relevant remittance advices**.

Date	Cheque No	Supplier	Amount	Details
22nd May	101333	Abacus C & C	369.60	Inv B/1874
22nd May	101334	Compugames	1005.60	Settle account in full.

TASK 8

Refer to the following cash sales and enter receipts into the computer. Use the bank current account for this transaction and enter 'cash sales' as the reference.

Date	Receipt Type	Gross	VAT	NET	Nominal code
13th May	Cash sale	1,200.00	200.00	1,000.00	4000
13th May	Cash sale	2,879.40	479.90	2,399.50	4001
20th May	Cash sale	995.00	0.00	995.00	4000

TASK 9

Enter the following petty cash payments onto the computerised accounting system.

Petty Cash Voucher	
Date:	20.05.XX
Voucher No:	012
Details	**£**
Subscriptions	32.00
(no Vat)	
Authorised By;	*James Free*
Receipt attached	

Petty Cash Voucher	
Date:	21.05.XX
Voucher No:	013
Details	**£**
Refreshments	10.40
VAT	2.08
Total	12.48
Authorised By;	*James Free*
Receipt attached	

TASK 10

Enter the following journal on the computerised accounting system.

Reference: JNL02			
Date	**Account Name & Code**	**Dr**	**Cr**
25th May	Drawings	2000.00	
	Bank		2000.00
Being the transfer of cash for James Free's personal use.			

TASK 11

Produce the following reports:

(a)   Trial Balance Report for May (including opening balances)

(b)   Sales Day Book

(c)   Sales Returns Day Book

(d)   Purchase Day Book

(e)   Customer Activity Report

(f)   Supplier Activity Report

(g)   Aged Creditors Report (Detailed)

(h)   Aged Debtors Report (Detailed)

TASK 12

Refer to the following email below from James Free.

E-Mail
From: James Free   **To:**   Accounts Technician   **Date:**   19th May 20XX   **Subject:**
Hello   A credit customer Forming Fun has moved premises. Their new address is as follows: 100 Aventi Way   St Albans   Hertfordshire   AL2 4PM   Please ensure that this is updated on the computerised accounts system.   Thanks   James

Create a screen shot of the customer's record with the new address and save it as a 'Word' document.

TASK 13

The sum of £502.00 has been incorrectly posted to the rent account instead of the electricity account in error. Process the following journal to correct this using reference JNL03. Use 31st May for the transaction.

Reference: JNL03			
Date	**Account Name & Code**	**Dr**	**Cr**
31st May	Electricity	502.00	
	Rent & Rates		502.00

Being the transfer of cash which was incorrectly posted to Rent instead of Electricity.

TASK 14

The following cheque payments were sent to suppliers; enter the payments on the accounts system and **produce the relevant remittance advices**.

Date	Supplier	Cheque No	Details	Amount
28th May	Space Models	101335	Payment of opening balance	306.00
28th May	Toys Unlimited	101336	Part payment invoice W/032	450.00
28th May	Abacus C & C	BACS	Payment of invoice B/989	540.00

TASK 15

The following payments were received from customers; enter the receipts on the accounts system, dated 29 May 20XX.

Customer	Cheque No	Details	Amount (£)
Busy Bee	104662	Invoice 2021	3102.00
Forming Fun	828100	Part payment invoice 2022	400.00
Teddy T's Party	672522	Payment of invoice 2023	6000.00

TASK 16

On 14th May a member of staff buys Computer Games paying you £264.00 in Cash. This is inclusive of 20% VAT. Enter this in the bank current account and use reference CSH41 for this transaction.

TASK 17

On 19th May, you sold a 'Jigsaw' to a customer and they paid £45.00 (Zero rated VAT) debit card. Enter this in the bank current account and use reference 'Debit Card' for this transaction.

TASK 18

On the 5th May you are asked to set up a monthly recurring payment for a Direct Debit. It is to pay Insurance for £100.00 (Exempt VAT) for a period of 12 months commencing on 31st May. There is no VAT on this transaction. Select/create/amend any ledger accounts. The Insurance is payable to Galloway Union. Provide evidence by taking a screen shot and saving it as a 'Word' document. Ensure you process this month's transaction.

TASK 19

You are asked to ensure that the petty cash account float is restored to a balance of £300.00 by bank transfer (dated 31st May). Enter this transaction onto the computerised system and use reference CSH25.

TASK 20

Toy Shop has been granted a bank loan for £10,000.00 and it has been received in to the bank current account on 31 May 20XX. Process the following journal to record this transaction (use ref JNL04).

Reference: JNL04			
Date	**Account Name & Code**	**Dr**	**Cr**
31st May	Bank Current Account	10000.00	
	Loan Account		10000.00

Being the proceeds received for a new loan.

TASK 21

You are given the following bank statement and are asked to produce a bank reconciliation as at 31st May, processing any adjustments that may be necessary.

Friendly Bank plc
201 Main Road
Rochester
Kent
ME15 9JP

Toy Shop
64 Long Lane
Langthorne   31st May 20XX
North Yorkshire   Statement no: 0003
YO21 3EJ

Account number: 00678432

Statement of Account

Date: May 20XX	Details	Paid out £	Paid in £	Balance £
1 May	Opening balance			4225.00C
1 May	Transfer	500.00		3725.00C
13 May	Counter credit		1200.00	4925.00C
13 May	Counter credit		2879.40	7804.40C
14 May	Counter credit		264.00	8068.40C
17 May	Counter credit		349.20	8417.60C
17 May	Counter credit		99.60	8517.20C
19 May	Debit Card		45.00	8562.20C
20 May	Counter credit		995.00	9557.20C
22 May	Cheque 101333	369.60		9187.60C
23 May	Cheque 101334	1005.60		8182.00C
25 May	Counter debit Ref: JNL 02	2000.00		6182.00C
26 May	BACS: Teddy's T Party		195.60	6377.60C
28 May	Cheque 101336	450.00		5927.60C
29 May	Counter credit		3102.00	9029.60C
29 May	Counter credit		6000.00	15029.60C
29 May	Counter credit		400.00	15429.60C
30 May	BACS payment	540.00		14889.60C
31 May	Transfer	44.48		14845.12C
31 May	Direct Debit – Galloway Union	100.00		14745.12C
31 May	Bank charges	101.32		14643.80C
31 May	Loan		10000.00	24643.80C
	D = Debit C = Credit			

TASK 22

Produce the following reports

(a)   Customer Activity (detailed) Report

(b)   Supplier Activity (detailed) Report

(c)   Period Trial Balance for the month of May (including opening balances)

(d)   Audit Trail for May (detailed – transactions only including bank reconciled & opening balances)

(e)   Aged Debtors (summary)

PRACTICE PAPER 2

CRAZY HAIR

THE SITUATION

This assignment is based on a new business, Crazy Hair, a small business recently set up to selling hair products.

The owner of the business is Nina Birk who operates as a sole trader.

At the start of the business Nina operated a manual bookkeeping system but has now decided that from 1st May 20XX the accounting system will become computerised.

You can assume that all documentation has been checked and authorised by Nina Birk.

Some nominal ledger accounts have already been allocated suitable account codes. **You may need to amend or create other account codes.**

Crazy Hair's financial year starts in May of the current year.

Their company details are:-

Crazy Hair

34 Clapham Road

Clapham

London

SE3 2HR

Tel: 01234 567891

You are employed as an accounting technician.

The business is registered for VAT. The rate of VAT charged on all goods and services sold by Crazy Hair is 20%. VAT registration number 123456789.

TASK 1

Refer to the customer listing below and set up customer records to open Sales Ledger accounts for each customer.

Customer account code	Customer name, address and contact details	Customer account details
104	Alfred Images Masuki Offices PO Box 5684 Birmingham B23 4RD	Credit limit: £8000 Payment Terms: 30 days Opening Balance: £1809.60 (relates to invoice 3352 dated 2nd April)
110	Figgaro Beta Studio 34 Knightsbridge Way Morden SE23 4KA	Credit limit: £6500 Payment Terms: 30 days Opening Balance: £3880.80 (relates to invoice 2856 dated 10th April)
118	Blades Alpha Studio 45 Key West London SE1 0JF	Credit limit: £6100 Payment Terms: 30 days Opening Balance: £2144.40 (relates to invoice 3345 dated 18th April)
122	Hair Studio Framlington Court Lee London SE4 7YH	Credit limit: £5000 Payment Terms: 30 days Opening Balance: £681.60 (relates to invoice 3098 dated 12th April)
138	Ribbons & Curls PO Box 1120 Canning Town London TN2 2EB	Credit limit: £5000 Payment Terms: 30 days Opening Balance: £391.20 (relates to invoice 3123 dated 12th April)

TASK 2

Refer to the supplier listing below and set up supplier records to open Purchase Ledger accounts for each supplier.

Supplier account code	Supplier name, address and contact details	Supplier account details
1134	Avada Cash & Carry 32 Surrey Quay Isle of Dogs E12 3NW	Credit limit: £5500 Payment Terms: 30 days Opening Balance: £4454.40 (relates to invoice C/251 dated 22nd April)
1138	Straightside Supplies Havering Place Holborn London WC1 2PP	Credit limit: £12000 Payment Terms: 30 days Opening Balance: £1839.60 (relates to invoice 9140 dated 11th April)
1165	Hair Supplies 43 St Helens Way London SE7 3RF	Credit limit: £4000 Payment Terms: 30 days Opening Balance: £818.40 (relates to invoice 0028 dated 11th April)
1185	Wig Specialists Retro Square 32 Wigmore Road London EC1V 3SG	Credit limit: £5000 Payment Terms: 30 days Opening Balance: £102.00 (relates to invoice S653 dated 18th April)

TASK 3.1

Refer to the list of General ledger balances below. Enter the opening balances into the computer, making sure you select/create/amend the appropriate general ledger account codes.

List of general ledger balances as at the **1st May**

Account name	£	£
Motor Vehicle	24000.00	
Furniture and Fixtures	31000.00	
Bank	54210.81	
Petty Cash	200.00	
Sales Ledger Control Account *	8907.60	
Purchase Ledger Control Account*		7214.40
VAT on Sales		5550.00
VAT on Purchases	1507.94	
Capital		165000.00
Drawings	5000.00	
Sales – Brushes		345.00
Sales – Combs		187.00
Sales – Colours		3801.45
Sales – Hairdryers		758.00
Sales – Wigs		5600.00
Cash Sales		617.50
Purchases – Brushes	873.00	
Purchases – Combs	50.00	
Purchases – Colour	4200.00	
Purchases – Hairdryers	6310.00	
Purchases – Wigs	52814.00	
*Note You do not need to enter these figures as you have already entered opening balances for customers and suppliers.		

TASK 3.2

Produce the following reports and **identify and correct any errors**:

(a)   Customer Address List

(b)   Supplier Address List

(c)   Trial Balance

TASK 4

Enter the following sales invoices onto the computer.

Crazy Hair	
34 Clapham Road	
Clapham	
London	
SE3 2HR	

Account No: 138
Invoice No: 3353

Date: 12 May 20XX

Ribbons & Curls
PO Box 1120
Canning Town
London
TN2 2EB

Quantity	Description	Unit Price	Net Cost	Tax	Gross	Nominal code
10	Colours	14.10	141.00	28.20	169.20	4002

Terms 30 days

Crazy Hair	
34 Clapham Road	
Clapham	
London	
SE3 2HR	

Account No: 104
Invoice No: 3354

Date: 12 May 20XX

Alfred Images
Masuki Offices
PO Box 5684
Birmingham
B23 4RD

Quantity	Description	Unit Price	Net Cost	Tax	Gross	Nominal code
50	Brushes	11.62	581.00	116.20	697.20	4000

Terms 30 days

Crazy Hair
34 Clapham Road
Clapham
London
SE3 2HR

Account No: 110
Invoice No: 3355

Date: 13th May 20XX

Figgaro
Beta Studio
34 Knightsbridge Way
Morden
SE23 4KA

Quantity	Description	Unit Price	Net Cost	Tax	Gross	Nominal code
12	Hairdryers	55.00	660.00	132.00	792.00	4003

Terms 30 days

Crazy Hair
34 Clapham Road
Clapham
London
SE3 2HR

Account No: 118
Invoice No: 3356

Date: 15th May 20XX

Blades
Alpha Studio
45 Key West
London
SE1 0JF

Quantity	Description	Unit Price	Net Cost	Tax	Gross	Nominal code
8	Wigs	210.72	1685.76	337.15	2022.91	4004
3	Hairdryers	67.80	203.40	40.68	244.08	4003

Terms 30 days

Crazy Hair
34 Clapham Road
Clapham
London
SE3 2HR

Account No: 122
Invoice No: 3357

Date: 18 May 20XX

Hair Studio
Framlington Court
Lee
London
SE4 7YH

Quantity	Description	Unit Price	Net Cost	Tax	Gross	Nominal code
12	Brushes	26.40	316.80	63.36	380.16	4000
4	Wigs	220.48	881.92	176.38	1058.30	4004
16	Colours	14.40	230.40	46.08	276.48	4002

Terms 30 days

TASK 5

On 25th May you send a credit note (CN23) to Alfred Images (Account No 104) for brushes.

The total is £67.20 which includes tax.

TASK 6

Enter the purchases invoices into the computer.

Date	A/C No.	Invoice Ref	Description	Nominal Code	Net	Vat	Gross
11 May	1138	3362	Brushes	5000	191.60	38.32	229.92
11 May	1134	C/910	Colours	5002	954.00	190.80	1144.80
13 May	1165	0814	Hairdryers	5003	178.56	0.00	178.56
14 May	1185	S1198	Wigs	5004	3393.60	678.72	4072.32

TASK 7

Enter the following purchase credit note onto the computer system.

Date	A/C No	Supplier	N/C	Credit Note Ref	Amount
18 May	1185	Wigs Specialist	5004	C3223	123.24 Including Vat

TASK 8

The following payments were received from customers; enter the receipts on the accounts system.

Date	Receipt type	Customer	Amount	Details
20 May	Cheque No: 183001	Alfred Images	1809.60	Payment for invoice 3352
21 May	Cheque No: 654255	Blades	2144.40	Payment for invoice 3345
21 May	BACS	Figgaro	3880.80	Payment for invoice 2856
21 May	Cheque No: 452221	Hair Studio	681.60	Payment for invoice 3098

TASK 9

The following cheque payments were sent to suppliers; enter the payments on the accounts system dated 31st May and **produce the relevant remittance advices**.

Supplier	Cheque No:	Amount	Details
Wigs Specialist	163455	£102.00	Payment for invoice S653
Avada Cash & Carry	163456	£4454.40	Payment for invoice C/251
Hair Supplies	163457	£818.40	Payment for invoice 0028

TASK 10

Enter the following petty cash payments into the computer. Check the nominal codes before entering the payments and select/create/amend any ledger accounts where necessary.

Date	Ref	Nominal Code	Net	VAT	Gross
19 May	CSH 86	7400	33.60	6.72	40.32
20 May	CSH 87	7500	4.51	0.00	4.51

TASK 11

On the 20th May, a member of staff purchases a 'Brush' from you and pays Crazy Hair a total of £21.00 in cash. This is inclusive of VAT of £3.50. Enter this in the bank current account and use reference 1001 for this transaction.

TASK 12

Produce the following reports:

(a)   Trial Balance Report

(b)   Sales Day Book

(c)   Sales Returns Day Book

(d)   Purchase Day Book

(e)   Customer Activity Report

(f)   Supplier Activity Report

(g)   Aged Creditors Report (summary)

(h)   Aged Debtors Report (summary)

TASK 13

Enter the following journal

<table>
<tr><th colspan="4">Ref : JH12</th></tr>
<tr><th>Date</th><th>Account Name & Code</th><th>Dr</th><th>Cr</th></tr>
<tr><td>24 May</td><td>Drawings</td><td>440.00</td><td></td></tr>
<tr><td></td><td>Bank</td><td></td><td>440.00</td></tr>
</table>

Being the transfer of cash for personal use.

TASK 14

(a)   Refer to the following email below from Frances Williams

E-Mail
From: Frances Williams
Date: 19th May 20XX
Subject: Customer change of address

Hello

A credit customer Ribbons and Curls has moved premises. New address as follows:

122 Devonshire Road

Cranbrook

London

SE1 2AB

Please ensure that this is updated on the computerised accounts system.

Thanks

Frances

(b)   **Create a screen shot** of the customer's record showing the change of address and save it as a 'Word' document. Use a suitable file name to save the document.

TASK 15

On 31st May you transfer £30.52 from the Bank account to the petty cash account. Use reference TRF01.

TASK 16

You are given the following bank statement and are asked to produce a bank reconciliation at 31st May, processing any adjustments that may be necessary. Ensure that the direct debit for Coopers Union is coded to Premises Insurance costs. Check the nominal codes list and select/create/amend any ledger accounts where necessary. There is no VAT applicable on both direct debits.

Nice Bank plc
201 Main Road
Rochester
Kent
ME15 9JP

Crazy Hair
34 Clapham Road
London
SE3 2HR

31st May 20XX
Statement no: 0012

Account number: 32543211

Statement of Account

Date: May 20XX	Details	Paid out £	Paid in £	Balance £
01 May	Opening balance			54210.81C
14 May	Counter credit		1809.60	56020.41C
20 May	Counter credit		2144.40	58164.81C
20 May	BACS		3880.80	62045.61C
20 May	Counter credit		681.60	62727.21C
20 May	Counter credit		21.00	62748.21C
24 May	Counter Debit	440.00		62308.21C
24 May	Direct Debit – Coopers Union	168.00		62140.11C
24 May	Counter Debit	30.52		62109.69C
31 May	Direct Debit – Electricity	66.94		62042.75C
31 May	Bank Charges	27.11		62015.64C
	D = Debit C = Credit			

TASK 17

Produce the following reports

(a)   Customer Address List

(b)   Customer Activity

(c)   Supplier Activity

(d)   Trial Balance for the month of May (include opening balances)

(e)   Audit Trail for May only (Detailed – including opening balances)

(f)   Aged Creditors (summary)

(g)   Aged Debtors (summary)

(h)   Nominal Ledger Activity Report for the following accounts

      1.1.1. Bank Current Account

      1.1.2. Petty Cash Account

PRACTICE PAPER 3

SHOES 4U

THE SITUATION

This assignment is based on an existing organisation, Shoes 4U, a small business selling ladies and men's shoes.

The owner of the business is Dennis Cope who operates as a sole trader.

At the start of the business Dennis operated a manual bookkeeping system but has now decided that from 1st June 20XX the accounting system will become computerised.

You can assume that all documentation has been checked by Dennis Cope.

Some nominal ledger accounts have already been allocated suitable account codes. **You may need to amend or create other account codes.**

Shoes 4U's financial year starts in June of the current year.

Their company details are:-

Shoes 4U

85 Barrington Close

Carlisle

Cumbria

C41 3ED

Tel: 01234 567891

You are employed as an accounting technician.

The business is registered for VAT. The rate of VAT charged on all goods and services sold by Shoes 4U is 20%. VAT registration number 123456789.

TASK 1

Refer to the customer listing below and set up customer records to open Sales Ledger accounts for each customer.

Customer account code	Customer name, address and contact details	Customer account details
SL186	Beckers Gate Ltd Butchergate Carlisle Cumbria C41 1SG	Credit limit: £5000 Payment Terms: 30 days Opening Balance: £4811.88 (relates to invoice 1613 dated 22nd May)
SL213	Eaton Bowls Club Seaton Street St Neots Cambs PE19 8EF	Credit limit: £3000 Payment Terms: 30 days Opening Balance: £961.98 (relates to invoice 1582 dated 10th May)
SL302	Jones Footwear Scotby Village Carlisle Cumbria C44 8BP	Credit limit: £6000 Payment Terms: 30 days Opening Balance: £3828.75 (relates to invoice 1596 dated 28th May)
SL307	Dickens Ladies Footwear 17 Royal Square Bleachfield North Yorkshire YO87 9AD	Credit limit: £11000 Payment Terms: 30 days Opening Balance: £783.66 (relates to invoice 1601 dated 21st May)

TASK 2

Refer to the supplier listing below and set up supplier records to open Purchase Ledger accounts for each supplier.

Supplier account code	Supplier name, address and contact details	Supplier account details
PL112	Bootsy & Smudge Ltd Factory Road Stilton Cambs PE7 3RP	Credit limit: £4000 Payment Terms: 30 days Opening Balance: £2881.26 (relates to invoice B/468 dated 22nd May)
PL168	Briggsthorpe Boots Long Buckby Wharf Long Buckby Northampton NN4 9UW	Credit limit: £50000 Payment Terms: 30 days Opening Balance: £43200.00 (relates to invoice 0001087 dated 18th May)
PL172	Gallows Fashion 18 The Crescent Pickford Cambs PE7 8QV	Credit limit: £2000 Payment Terms: 30 days Opening Balance: £400.00 (relates to invoice G-01239 dated 16th May)
PL173	Dickens Ladies Footwear 17 Royal Square Bleachfield North Yorkshire YO87 9AD	Credit limit: £2000 Payment Terms: 30 days Opening Balance: £567.00 (relates to invoice 06345 dated 16th May)

KAPLAN PUBLISHING

TASK 3.1

Refer to the list of General ledger balances below. Enter the opening balances into the computer, making sure you select/create/amend the appropriate general ledger account codes.

List of general ledger balances as at the 1st June

Account name	£	£
Freehold Property	72000.00	
Motor Vehicles	7500.00	
Furniture and Fixtures	9000.00	
Bank	19363.00	
Petty Cash	200.00	
Sales Ledger Control *	10386.27	
Purchase Ledger Control *		47048.26
VAT on Sales		3402.35
VAT on Purchases	1130.00	
Capital		30000.00
Drawings	600.00	
Sales – Men's Footwear		79320.00
Sales – Ladies Footwear		43210.00
Cash Sales		6798.00
Purchases – Men's Footwear	55432.00	
Purchases – Ladies Footwear	23410.00	
Advertising	7231.00	
Telephone	866.00	
Rent	1263.00	
Electricity	567.34	
Office Stationery	830.00	
*Note You do not need to enter these figures as you have already entered opening balances for customers and suppliers		

TASK 3.2

Transfer £5000 from the bank current account to the bank deposit account, dated 1st June. Use TRF01 as the reference.

TASK 3.3

Produce the following reports and identify and correct any errors:

(a)   Customer Address list

(b)   Supplier Address List

(c)   Period Trial Balance Report

TASK 4

Enter the following sales invoices and credit notes on to the computer.

Shoes 4u
85 Barrington Close
Carlisle
Cumbria
C41 3ED

Sales Invoice No: 1622
Date: 4th June 20XX

Becker Gate Ltd
Butchergate
Carlisle
Cumbria
C41 1SG

Description	£
Men's Footwear	450.00
VAT @ 20.00%	90.00
Total for payment	540.00

Terms 30 days

Shoes 4u
85 Barrington Close
Carlisle
Cumbria
C41 3ED

Sales Invoice No: 1623
Date: 6th June 20XX

Eaton Bowls Club
Seaton Street
St Neots
Cambs
PE19 8EF

Description	£
Men's Footwear	1385.00
VAT @ 20.00%	277.00
Total for payment	1662.00

Terms 30 days

Shoes 4u
85 Barrington Close
Carlisle
Cumbria
C41 3ED

Sales Invoice No: 1624
Date: 14th June 20XX

Dickens Ladies Footwear
17 Royal Square
Bleachfield
North Yorkshire
YO87 9AD

Description	£
Men's Footwear	450.00
Ladies Footwear	1850.00
VAT @ 20.00%	460.00
Total for payment	2760.00

Terms 30 days

Shoes 4u
85 Barrington Close
Carlisle
Cumbria
C41 3ED

Sales Invoice No: 1625
Date: 17th June 20XX

Jones Footwear
Scotby Village
Carlisle
Cumbria
C44 8BP

Description	£
Ladies Footwear	1175.75
VAT @ 20.00%	235.15
Total for payment	1410.90

Terms 30 days

Shoes 4u
85 Barrington Close
Carlisle
Cumbria
C41 3ED

Credit Note No: CR10
Date: 8th June 20XX

Dickens Ladies Footwear

17 Royal Square

Bleachfield

North Yorkshire

YO87 9AD

Description	£
Returned Ladies Footwear – Damage in transit	235.00
VAT @ 20.00%	47.00
Total for payment	282.00

Terms 30 days

TASK 5

Enter supplier invoices into the computer.

Date	Description	N/C	Invoice Ref	Net	Vat	Gross
2 June	Bootsy & Smudge Ltd	5001	B/752	300.00	60.00	360.00
10 June	Briggsthorpe Boots	5000	12350	2500.00	500.00	3000.00
12 June	Gallows Fashion	5000	G-2285	2500.00	500.00	3000.00
13 June	Bootsy & Smudge Ltd	5001	B/753	200.00	40.00	240.00

TASK 6

The following payments were received from customers; enter the receipts on the accounts system.

Date	A/c No	Customer	Cheque No	Details	Amount £
11 June	SL186	Beckers Gate Ltd	199846	Payment for invoice 1613	4811.88
14 June	SL213	Eaton Bowls Club	107654	Payment for invoice 1582	961.98
14 June	SL302	Jones Footwear	244536	Payment for invoice 1596	3828.75

TASK 7

The following cheque payments were sent to suppliers; enter the payments on the accounts system and **raise the relevant remittance advices**.

Date	A/c No	Supplier	Cheque No	Details	Amount £
18 June	PL172	Gallows Fashion	109887	Payment for invoice G-01239	400.00
18 June	PL168	Briggsthorpe Boots	109888	Part Payment for invoice 0001087	23300.00

TASK 8.1

The following items were paid by cash

Petty Cash Voucher	
Date:	05.06.XX
Voucher No:	010
Details	£
Refreshments (no Vat)	9.90
Authorised By;	*Dennis Cope*
Receipt attached	

Petty Cash Voucher	
Date:	10.06.XX
Voucher No:	011
Details	£
Office stationery	11.25
VAT	2.25
Total	13.50
Authorised By;	*Dennis Cope*
Receipt attached	

TASK 8.2

Reimburse the petty cash tin with £23.40 which has been withdrawn from the bank. Use 10th June 20XX and reference TRF02 for this transaction.

TASK 9

On the 23rd June, a member of staff purchases 'Mens Footwear' from you and pays you a total of £77.59 in cash. This is inclusive of VAT. Enter this in to the bank current account and use reference F027 for the transaction.

TASK 10

Produce the following reports:

(1)   Trial Balance Report

(2)   Sales Day Book

(3)   Customer Activity Report

(4)   Supplier Activity Report

(5)   Aged Creditors Report (detailed)

(6)   Aged Debtors Report (detailed)

(7)   Nominal Ledger Activity Report for the following accounts

        (a)   Bank Current Account

        (b)   Petty Cash Account

TASK 11.1

Refer to the following standing order schedule:

- Set up a recurring entry as shown in the standing order schedule below.
- **Produce a screen shot** of the screen setting up the recurring entry.
- Process the first payment.

Details	Amount	Frequency of payment	Total number of payments	Payment start date 20XX	Payment finish date 20XX
Electricity (ECBE Ltd)	£193.00 No Vat	Quarterly	4	25th June 20XX	25th March 20XX

TASK 11.2

Refer to the following BACS receipt schedule:

- Set up a recurring entry as shown in the schedule below.
- **Produce a screen shot** of the screen setting up the recurring entry.
- Process the first receipt.

Details	Amount	Frequency of receipt	Total number of receipts	Start date 20XX	Finish date 20XX
Rent	£1500 (no VAT)	Quarterly	4	25th June 20XX	25th March 20XX

TASK 12

Enter the following journal.

JOURNAL No: 209			
Date	**Account Name & Code**	**Dr**	**Cr**
25th June	Drawings	3200.00	
	Bank		3200.00

Being the transfer of cash for personal use.

TASK 13

On 22nd June you sold Ladies Footwear to a customer and they paid £54.00 debit card inclusive of tax £9.00. Use reference DC03.

TASK 14

You are given the following bank statement and are asked to produce a bank reconciliation at 30th June 20XX, processing any adjustments that may be necessary. The BACS receipt on the 25th June relates to Rent Received.

Friendly Bank plc

201 Lake Rise
Whitewater
Cumbria
C21 9JF

STATEMENT : ACCOUNT No 22567767

Shoes 4U
85 Barrington Close
Carlisle
Cumbria
C41 3ED

30th June 20XX
Statement 0011

Date June 20XX	Detail	Paid out £	Paid in £	Balance
1st June	Opening Balance			19363.00C
1st June	Transfer	5000.00		14363.00C
14th June	Counter debit	23.40		14339.60C
14th June	Cheque receipt		4811.88	19151.48C
14th June	Cheque receipt		961.98	20113.46C
18th June	Cheque 109888	23300.00		3186.54D
21st June	Debit Card transaction		54.00	3132.54D
22nd June	DD – ECBE Ltd	193.00		3325.54D
23rd June	Counter credit		77.59	3247.95D
25th June	Counter Debit	3200.00		6447.95D
25th June	Bank Charges	50.00		6497.95D
25th June	BACS receipt		1500.00	4997.95D
30th June	Counter Credit		3828.75	1169.20D

C = Credit	D = Debit	DD – Direct Debit

TASK 15

Produce the following reports:

(1)   Trial Balance for the month of June (Inc. opening balances)

(2)   Detailed Audit Trail (including bank reconciled items)

(3)   Nominal Ledger Activity Report for the following accounts:

    (a)   Trade Creditors

    (b)   Sales – Ladies Footwear

(4)   Aged Debtors Analysis (detailed)

PRACTICE PAPER 4

SPORTS GEAR

THE SITUATION

This assignment is based on an existing business, **Sports Gear**, who has recently set up in business selling sports equipment.

The owner of the business is Nina Birk who operates as a sole trader.

At the start of the business Nina operated a manual bookkeeping system but has now decided that from 1st July 20XX the accounting system will become computerised.

You can assume that all documentation has been checked and authorised by Nina Birk.

Some nominal ledger accounts have already been allocated suitable account codes. **You may need to amend or create other account codes.**

Sport Gear's Financial Year starts in July.

Their company details are:-

Sports Gear

34 Hockey Avenue

Tennison

London

EC1V 1NY

Tel: 01234 567891

You are employed as an accounting technician.

The business is registered for VAT. The rate of VAT charged on all goods and services sold by Sports Gear is 20%. VAT registration number 123456789.

TASK 1

Refer to the customer listing below and set up customer records to open Sales Ledger accounts for each customer.

Customer account code	Customer name, address and contact details	Customer account details
SL01	J Hollingham 56 Glencoe Avenue Gants Hill Ilford Essex IG1 6FR	Credit limit: £5000 Payment Terms: 30 days Opening Balance: £3462.12 (relates to invoice 1001 dated 12th June 20XX)
SL02	Paul McCallum 34 St Albans Road Seven Kings Essex IG7 8DS	Credit limit: £9500 Payment Terms: 30 days Opening Balance: £514.68 (relates to invoice 0087 dated 10th June 20XX)
SL03	Kerry Jenkins 34 Gloucester Road Gillingham Kent ME14 3TL	Credit limit: £8000 Payment Terms: 30 days Opening Balance: £758.34 (relates to invoice 0093 dated 8th June 20XX)
SL04	Harry Bucket 54 Dale Road Harrogate North Yorks YO2 3HN	Credit limit: £12000 Payment Terms: 30 days Opening Balance: £2767.34 (relates to invoice 1003 dated 12th June 20XX)
SL05	Evelyn Rose 98 Crabtree Drive Bromley Kent DA3 6AY	Credit limit: £7000 Payment Terms: 30 days Opening Balance: £942.98 (relates to invoice 1004 dated 12th June 20XX)

TASK 2

Refer to the supplier listing below and set up supplier records to open Purchase Ledger account for each supplier.

Supplier account code	Supplier name, address and contact details	Supplier account details
PL01	Radcliff and Sons Orient House Lower Clapham London E1 2RH	Credit limit: £15500 Payment Terms: 30 days Opening Balance: £5362.14 (relates to invoice 1874 dated 22nd June 20XX)
PL02	Tennison Bros White Cottage London WC1 6YD	Credit limit: £11000 Payment Terms: 30 days Opening Balance: £2801.00 (relates to invoice B-321 dated 11th June 20XX)
PL03	Skipton & Co 22 Chatsworth Lane Water Square London EC1V 6NJ	Credit limit: £9000 Payment Terms: 30 days Opening Balance: £501.00 (relates to invoice 1087 dated 11th June 20XX)
PL04	Evelyn Rose 98 Crabtree Drive Bromley Kent DA3 6AY	Credit limit: £3000 Payment Terms: 30 days Opening Balance: £250.00 (relates to invoice A193 dated 18th June 20XX)

TASK 3.1

Refer to the list of General ledger balances below. Enter the opening balances into the computer, making sure you select/create/amend any ledger accounts where necessary.

List of general ledger balances as at 01.07.20XX

Account name	£	£
Motor Vehicle	15500.00	
Furniture and Fixtures	18000.00	
Office Equipment	8430.00	
Bank	3325.40	
Petty Cash	300.00	
Sales Ledger Control Account*	8445.46	
Purchase Ledger Control Account*		8914.14
VAT on Sales		3458.00
VAT on Purchases	1120.00	
Capital		52000.00
Drawings	1294.00	
Sales – Tennis Racquets		13266.78
Sales – Exercise Bikes		22310.00
Sales – Golf Clubs		9543.00
Sales – Fishing Rods		5644.00
Purchases – Tennis Racquets	21354.00	
Purchases – Exercise Bikes	25610.00	
Purchases – Golf Clubs	5475.00	
Purchases – Fishing Rods	4796.00	
Office Stationery	430.00	
Postage	560.00	
Electricity	496.06	
Note You do not need to enter these figures as you have already entered opening balances for customers and suppliers		

TASK 3.2

Produce the following reports and **identify and correct any errors:**

- Customer Address list

- Supplier Address List

- Period Trial Balance Report

TASK 4

Enter the following sales invoices and credit notes onto the computer.

INVOICE

Sports Gear

34 Hockey Avenue

Tennison

London

EC1V 1NY

Account No: SL01   Date: 4 July 20XX

Invoice No: 1052

J Hollingham

56 Glencoe Avenue

Gants Hill

Ilford

Essex

IG1 6FR

Quantity	Description	Unit Price	Net £	Tax £	Gross £	Nominal code
20	Tennis Racquets	44.10	882.00	176.40	1058.40	4000
10	Exercise Bikes	102.36	1023.60	204.72	1228.32	4001
6	Fishing Rods	54.00	324.00	64.80	388.80	4003

Terms 30 days

INVOICE

Sports Gear

34 Hockey Avenue

Tennison

London

EC1V 1NY

Account No: SL03   Date: 6 July 20XX

Invoice No: 1053

Kerry Jenkins

Gloucester Road

Gillingham

Kent

ME14 3TL

Quantity	Description	Unit Price	Net £	Tax £	Gross £	Nominal code
3	Tennis Racquets	44.10	132.30	26.46	158.76	4000

Terms 30 days

INVOICE

Sports Gear

34 Hockey Avenue

Tennison

London

EC1V 1NY

Account No: SL04   Date: 8 July 20XX

Invoice No: 1054

Harry Bucket

54 Dale Road

Yorkshire

Y02 3HN

Quantity	Description	Unit Price	Net £	Tax £	Gross £	Nominal code
18	Golf Clubs	84.10	1513.80	302.76	1816.56	4002

Terms 30 days

CREDIT NOTE

Sports Gear

34 Hockey Avenue

Tennison

London

EC1V 1NY

Account No: SL01   Date: 17 July 20XX

Invoice No: CR34

J Hollingham

56 Glencoe Avenue

Gants Hill

Ilford

Essex

IG1 6FR

Description	**£**
Return faulty Exercise Bike	510.63
VAT @ 20.0%	102.12
Total credit	612.75

TASK 5

Enter the purchases invoices into the computer. Check the nominal codes before entering the invoices and create/amend any ledger accounts where necessary.

Date	A/C No.	Invoice Ref	Description	Net	Vat	Gross	Nominal code
3 July	PL01	1099	Tennis Racquets	550.00	110.00	660.00	5000
5 July	PL02	B – 1147	Exercise Bikes	320.00	64.00	384.00	5001
5 July	PL02	B – 1147	Postage	35.00	0.00	35.00	7510
10 July	PL03	2785	Golf Clubs	938.00	187.60	1125.60	5002
10 July	PL04	A/5698	Fishing Rods	671.00	134.20	805.20	5003

TASK 6

On 19th July, you receive a credit note (CX432) from Skipton & Co (Account No PL03) for two Golf Clubs that had been returned to them. The total credit note is for 109.45 plus sales tax of 20%.

TASK 7

The following payments were received from customers; enter the receipts on the accounts system.

Date	Receipt type	Customer	Amount	Details
19 July	Cheque No. 542321	J Hollingham	2849.37	Payment for invoice 1001 including credit note CR34
12 July	Cheque No. 222547	Kerry Jenkins	758.34	Payment for invoice 0093
13 July	BACS	Harry Bucket	2767.34	Payment for invoice 1003

TASK 8

The following cheque payments were sent to suppliers; enter the payments on the accounts system and **raise the relevant remittance advices.**

Date	Cheque No:	Supplier	Amount	Details
14th July	170012	Radcliff & Sons	5362.14	Payment for invoice 1874
17th July	170013	Tennison Bros	2801.00	Payment for invoice B-321

TASK 9

Enter the Petty cash payments into the computer

Petty Cash Voucher	
Date:	10.07.XX
Voucher No:	152
Details	£
Stationery (no Vat)	19.90
Authorised By;	*Nina Birk*
Receipt attached	

Petty Cash Voucher	
Date:	20.07.XX
Voucher No:	187
Details	£
Postage	343.55
VAT	68.71
Total	412.26
Authorised By;	*Nina Birk*
Receipt attached	

TASK 10

Refer to the following cash sales and enter receipts into the bank current account on the computer.

Date	Receipt ref	Gross	VAT	NET	Nominal code
13 July	REC101	1,200.00	200.00	1,000.00	4000
15 July	REC102	2,879.40	479.90	2,399.50	4001
15 July	REC103	1,194.90	199.15	995.75	4000

TASK 11

Produce the following reports:

- Trial Balance Report
- Sales Day Book
- Purchase Day Book
- Customer Activity Report
- Supplier Activity Report
- Aged Creditors Report
- Aged Debtors Report
- Produce a Statement for Paul McCallum

TASK 12

Enter the following journal

Ref : JNL004			
Date	Account Name & Code	Dr	Cr
25.07.XX	Drawings	3,441.00	
	Bank		3,441.00

Being the transfer of cash for personal use.

TASK 13

Refer to the following email below from Nina Birk and **save a screenshot of your work** and save with a **suitable file name**.

E-Mail
From: Nina Birk
Date: 19th July 20XX
Subject: Customer change of address

Hello

A credit customer Harry Bucket has moved premises. New address as follows:

137 Chester Road

Capel Corner

CR3 2SA

Telephone: 08459 754 256

Please ensure that this is updated on the computerised accounts system.

Thanks

Nina

TASK 14

The following cheque payments were sent to suppliers; enter the payments on the accounts system.

Date	A/c No	Supplier	Cheque No	Details	Amount
28 July	PL03	Skipton & Co	170014	Invoice 1087	501.00
28 July	PL01	Radcliff & Sons	170015	Invoice 1099	660.00

TASK 15

The following payments were received from customers; enter the receipts on the accounts system.

Date	Customer	Cheque No	Details	Amount (£)
28 July	J Hollingham	087651	Invoice 1052	2675.52
28 July	Harry Bucket	198871	Invoice 1054	Part Payment of 500.00

TASK 16

On 14th July a member of staff buys a Tennis Racquet paying you £50.00 in Cash. This is inclusive of sales tax. Enter this in to the bank current account and use reference ST5 for the transaction.

TASK 17

On 19th July, you sold a 'Golf Club' to a customer and they paid £45.00 (Plus VAT) debit card. Use reference CS03.

TASK 18

You are asked to set up a monthly standing order for Insurance for £100.00 (Exempt VAT) for a period of 12 months commencing on 28th July. There is no VAT on this transaction. The Insurance is payable to Ipswich Union. Choose a suitable nominal code for Insurance. **Take a screenshot** of the details and save as a 'Word' document with a suitable file name. Process July's payment.

TASK 19

You are given the following bank statement and are asked to produce a bank reconciliation at 31st July, processing any adjustments that may be necessary.

Sully Bank plc
201 Main Road
Gillingham
Kent
ME3 5TF

Sports Gear
34 Hockey Avenue
Tennison
London
EC1V 1NY

31st July 20XX
Statement no: 1001

Account number 00678432

Statement of Account

Date: July 2011	Details	Paid out £	Paid in £	Balance £
01 July	Opening balance			3325.40C
12 July	Counter Credit		758.34	4083.74C
13 July	BACS		2767.34	6851.08C
13 July	Counter credit		1200.00	8051.08C
14 July	Counter credit		50.00	8101.08C
15 July	Counter credit		2879.40	10980.48C
15 July	Counter credit		1194.90	12175.38C
19 July	Cheque 170013	2801.00		9374.38C
20 July	Counter Credit		2849.37	12223.75C
20 July	Debit Card		54.00	12277.75C
25 July	Counter Debit	3441.00		8836.75C
29 July	Counter Credit		2675.52	11512.27C
29 July	Counter Credit		500.00	12012.27C
29 July	Standing Order – Ipswich Union	100.00		11912.27C
31 July	Bank charges	32.19		11880.08C
	D = Debit C = Credit			

TASK 20

Transfer £432.16 from the bank current account to the petty cash account. Use reference TRF01 for this transaction and date it 31st July.

TASK 21

Produce the following reports

- Customer Address List
- Customer Activity (detailed report)
- Supplier Activity (detailed report)
- Period Trial Balance for the month of July (inc. opening balances)
- Nominal Ledger Activity Report for the following accounts
  - Bank Current Account
  - Petty Cash Account

PRACTICE PAPER 5

WAY TO WORK

THE SITUATION

This assignment is based on an existing business, Way to Work.

At the start of the business they operated under a manual bookkeeping system but they have now decided that from 1st March 20XX the accounting system will become computerised.

Some nominal ledger accounts have already been allocated suitable account codes. **You may need to amend or create other account codes.**

Way to Work's financial year starts in March.

Their company details are:-

Way to Work

55 Upper Street

London

N1 9PE

Tel: 01234 567891

You are employed as an accounting technician.

The business is registered for VAT. The company's products are standard rated for VAT (20%). VAT registration number 123456789.

Set the company's financial year to start in March 20XX

TASK 1

Refer to the customer listing below and set up customer records to open Sales Ledger accounts for each customer.

Customer account code	Customer name, address and contact details	Customer account details
JP01	Morgan, Smith & Winston City Road Islington London N1 9PL	Credit limit: £7000 Payment Terms: 30 days Opening Balance: £1172.34 (relates to invoice INV021 dated 14th February 20XX)
JP02	Cyril West Grays West Grays Inn Road London WC1 1LT	Credit limit: £8500 Payment Terms: 30 days Opening Balance: £2954.00 (relates to invoice INV045 dated 22nd February 20XX).
JP03	Wallace & Gromit Ltd 134 Upper Street Islington London N1 2PT	Credit limit: £17000 Payment Terms: 30 days Opening Balance: £3180.00 (relates to invoice INV033 dated 18th February 20XX)
JP04	Star Paper 66 White Lion Street London N1 5RX	Credit limit: £12500 Payment Terms: 30 days Opening Balance: £1867.34 (relates to invoice INV034 dated 22nd February 20XX)

TASK 2

Refer to the supplier listing below and set up supplier records to open Purchase Ledger accounts for each supplier.

Supplier account code	Supplier name, address and contact details	Supplier account details
SP01	Paper Products UK South Down Trading Estate Sheffield S15 4DR	Credit limit: £8500 Payment Terms: 30 days Opening Balance: £445.23 (relates to invoice 0165 dated 28th February 20XX).
SP02	Wallace & Gromit Ltd 134 Upper Street Islington London N1 2PT	Credit limit: £12000 Payment Terms: 30 days Opening Balance: £6711.00 (relates to invoice 02183 dated 11th February 20XX)
SP03	Whole Office Furniture 176 East Way Leeds LD4 6PP	Credit limit: £4000 Payment Terms: 30 days Opening Balance: £1875.21 (relates to invoice 1028 dated 26th February 20XX)
SP04	Stationery World 32 Great Portland Road London WC1V 6HH	Credit limit: £16500 Payment Terms: 30 days Opening Balance: £9504.32 (relates to invoice 0187 dated 18th February 20XX).

TASK 3.1

Refer to the list of General ledger balances below. Enter the opening balances into the computer, making sure you select/create/amend the appropriate general ledger account codes.

List of general ledger balances as at 01.03.20XX

Account name	£	£
Motor Vehicle	14000.00	
Furniture and Fixtures	8000.00	
Bank	6210.81	
Petty Cash	100.00	
Sales Ledger Control Account *	9173.68	
Purchase Ledger Control Account*		18535.76
Capital		34000.00
Drawings	1000.00	
Stationery Sales		903.73
CD Roms Sales		855.00
Printer Accessories Sales		9842.00
Stationery purchases	2400.00	
CD Rom purchases	210.00	
Printer Accessory purchases	15000.00	
Wages and Salaries	5600.00	
General Expenses	342.00	
Rent	2100.00	
*Note You do not need to enter these figures as you have already entered opening balances for customers and suppliers.		

TASK 3.2

Transfer £1500.00 from the bank current account to the bank deposit account. Date the transaction 1st March and use reference TRANS01.

TASK 3.3

Produce the following reports and **identify and correct any errors**.

- Customer Address List
- Supplier Address List
- Trial Balance

TASK 4

Enter the sales invoices onto the computer.

Date	A/C No.	Invoice Ref	Description	Nominal Code	Gross £	VAT £	Net £
3 Mar	JP02	INV041	Stationery	4000	936.00	156.00	780.00
3 Mar	JP04	INV042	CD Roms	4001	1105.20	184.20	921.00
5 Mar	JP01	INV043	Printer Accessory	4002	5251.20	875.20	4376.00
7 Mar	JP03	INV044	Printer Accessory	4002	549.60	91.60	458.00
7 Mar	JP01	INV045	Stationery	4000	7452.00	1242.00	6210.00

TASK 5

On 17th March you send a credit note (CR51) to Star Paper (Account No JP04) for Printer Accessories.

The total is £251.27 plus tax.

TASK 6

Enter the purchases invoices into the computer.

Date	A/C No.	Invoice Ref	Description	Nominal Code	Gross	Vat	Net
10 Mar	SP01	0200	Stationery	5000	586.80	97.80	489.00
11 Mar	SP02	02241	CD Roms	5001	414.00	69.00	345.00
11 Mar	SP03	1098	Printer Accessory	5002	9153.60	1525.60	7628.00
14 Mar	SP04	0197	Stationery	5000	4280.40	713.40	3567.00

TASK 7

Enter the following purchase credit note onto the computer system.

Date	A/C No	Supplier	N/C	Credit Note Ref	Amount	Details
19 Mar	SP04	Stationery World	5000	RF287	124.08	Plus Tax

TASK 8

The following payments were received from customers; enter the receipts on the accounts system.

Date	Cheque Number	Customer	Amount	Details
15 Mar	203998	Morgan, Smith & Winston	1172.34	Payment for invoice INV021
17 Mar	103112	Cyril West	2954.00	Payment for invoice INV045
19 Mar	011211	Star Paper	1565.82	Payment for invoice INV034 including credit note CR51

TASK 9

The following cheque payments were sent to suppliers; enter the payments on the accounts system dated 31st March, and **raise the relevant remittance advices**.

Supplier	Cheque No:	Amount	Details
Paper Products UK	100076	445.23	Payment for invoice 0165
Whole Office Furniture	100077	1875.21	Payment for invoice 1028
Stationery World	100078	9504.32	Payment for invoice 0187

TASK 10

On 15th March you transfer £600.00 from the Bank account to the Petty Cash account. Use reference TRANS02 for this transaction.

TASK 11

Enter the following petty cash payments into the computer. Check the nominal codes before entering the payments and select/create/amend any ledger accounts where necessary.

Date	Ref	Nominal Code	Details	Net	VAT	Gross
19 Mar	056	7200	Electricity	84.10	16.82	100.92
20 Mar	057	6201	Advertising	327.00	65.40	392.40

TASK 12

On the 28th March, a member of staff purchases a 'Printer Accessories' from you and pays you a total of £123.48 in cash. This is inclusive of VAT of £20.58. Use reference ST4 for this transaction and enter the funds in to the bank current account.

TASK 13

On the 31st March you are asked to set up a monthly standing order for Rent for £568.00 (Exempt VAT) for a period of 12 months commencing on 31st March. The Rent is payable to ICPW Bank. Process the payment for March.

TASK 14

You are given the following bank statement and are asked to produce a bank reconciliation at 31st March, processing any adjustments that may be necessary.

<table>
<tr><td colspan="4">**Islington Bank Plc**
201 Upper Street
Islington
London
N1 9PE</td></tr>
<tr><td colspan="4">Way to Work
55 Upper Street
London
N1 9PE</td></tr>
<tr><td colspan="4">31st March 20XX
Statement no: 0002</td></tr>
<tr><td colspan="4">Account number: 32543211</td></tr>
<tr><td colspan="4">**Statement of Account**</td></tr>
</table>

Date: March 20XX	Details	Paid out £	Paid in £	Balance £
01 Mar	Opening balance			6210.81C
01 Mar	Transfer	1500.00		4710.81C
15 Mar	Transfer	600.00		4110.81C
18 Mar	Counter Credit		1172.34	5283.15C
18 Mar	Counter Credit		2954.00	8237.15C
19 Mar	Counter Credit		1565.82	9802.97C
26 Mar	100017	1875.21		7927.76C
28 Mar	Counter credit		123.48	8051.24C
31 Mar	100076	445.23		7606.01C
31 Mar	Standing Order – ICPW Bank	568.00		7038.01C
31 Mar	Bank Charges	123.45		6914.56C
	D = Debit C = Credit			

TASK 15

Produce the following reports

- Customer Activity (detailed report)
- Supplier Activity (detailed report)
- Trial Balance for the month of March (including opening balances)
- Audit Trial for March only (inc opening balances)
- Nominal Ledger Activity Report for the following accounts
  - Bank Current Account
  - Petty Cash Account

Section 2

ANSWERS TO PRACTICE QUESTIONS

PRACTICE PAPER 1

TOY SHOP ANSWERS

TASK 3.3

Customer Address List

	Toy Shop Customer Address List						20 Apr 2017 13:51

Address Types: All

Customer Name	Address	Contact name	Phone	Mobile	Email	Fax
Busy Bee Toys (BB01)	832 High Street Oxford OX2 3WG	Main Contact				
Forming Fun (FF02)	21 Newton Quay Knott Mill Manchester M6 3RJ	Main Contact				
Space Models (SM03)	13 Central Street Perth Scotland SC4 8RQ	Main Contact				
Teddy T's Party (TP04)	3 Paradise Street Wokingham WO4 6QP	Main Contact				

TASK 3.3

Supplier Address List

		Toy Shop			20 Apr 2017	
		Supplier Address List			13:53	

Address Types: All

Supplier Name	Address	Contact name	Phone	Mobile	Email	Fax
Abacus C & C (PL01)	Unit 31 Kitts Industrial Estate St Helens Lancs	Main Contact				
Compugames Ltd (PL02)	6 Jury Road Dublin Eire	Main Contact				
Space Models (PL03)	13 Central Street Perth Scotland	Main Contact				
Toys Unlimited (PL04)	95 Cuscaden Road Edinburgh Scotland	Main Contact				

TASK 3.3

Period Trial Balance Report

From: 30/04/2016
To: 30/04/2017

Toy Shop
Trial Balance Report

20 Apr 2017
13:57

This period only

Nominal Code	Name	Selected Period	
		Debit	Credit
0040	Fixtures and fittings - Cost	5,800.00	
0050	Motor Vehicles - Cost	3,000.00	
1100	Trade Debtors	2,223.60	
1200	Current	3,725.00	
1210	Cash	300.00	
1220	Deposit	500.00	
2100	Trade Creditors		2,157.60
2200	VAT on Sales		543.00
2201	VAT on Purchases	109.00	
3200	Capital introduced		20,000.00
3260	Drawings - equity	355.00	
4000	Sales - Computer Games		6,080.00
4001	Sales - Jigsaws		700.00
4002	Sales - Boxed Games		1,967.00
5000	Purchases - Computer Games	8,000.00	
5001	Purchases - Jigsaws	3,200.00	
5002	Purchases - Boxed Games	2,465.00	
7100	Rent and rates	1,550.00	
7200	Electricity	167.00	
7500	Office Stationery	53.00	
	TOTAL	£31,447.60	£31,447.60

TASK 7

Abacus C & C – remittance advice

Remittance Advice

Date Paid: 22/05/2016

Reference: PL01

Abacus C & C Unit 31 Kitts Industrial Estate St Helens Lancs	**Toy Shop** 64 Long Lane Langhorne North Yorkshire YO21 3EJ United Kingdom

Telephone: 01234 567891

VAT Number: GB 123456789

Reference: Chq no 101333

Our Ref	Your Ref	Date	Total Amount	Amount Paid
Inv B/1874		30/04/2016	369.60	369.60
			Total Paid:	**£ 369.60 GBP**

Compugames – remittance advice

Remittance Advice

Date Paid: 22/05/2016

Reference: PL02

Compugames Ltd 6 Jury Road Dublin Eire	**Toy Shop** 64 Long Lane Langhorne North Yorkshire YO21 3EJ United Kingdom

Telephone: 01234 567891

VAT Number: GB 123456789

Reference: Chq no 101334

Our Ref	Your Ref	Date	Total Amount	Amount Paid
Inv 1087		30/04/2016	511.20	511.20
145215		05/05/2016	600.00	600.00
CR 11245		15/05/2016	-105.60	-105.60
			Total Paid:	**£ 1,005.60 GBP**

TASK 11

Trial Balance Report

From: 30/04/2016
To: 31/05/2016

Toy Shop
Trial Balance Report

20 Apr 2017
15:29

This period only

Nominal Code	Name	Selected Period	
		Debit	Credit
0040	Fixtures and fittings - Cost	5,800.00	
0050	Motor Vehicles - Cost	3,000.00	
1100	Trade Debtors	10,897.20	
1200	Current	6,068.60	
1210	Cash	255.52	
1220	Deposit	500.00	
2100	Trade Creditors		3,034.80
2200	VAT on Sales		2,775.90
2201	VAT on Purchases	483.48	
3200	Capital introduced		20,000.00
3260	Drawings - equity	2,355.00	
4000	Sales - Computer Games		15,340.00
4001	Sales - Jigsaws		3,099.50
4002	Sales - Boxed Games		2,467.00
5000	Purchases - Computer Games	9,362.00	
5001	Purchases - Jigsaws	3,218.00	
5002	Purchases - Boxed Games	2,965.00	
7100	Rent and rates	1,550.00	
7200	Electricity	167.00	
7500	Office Stationery	53.00	
8201	Subscriptions	32.00	
8205	Refreshments	10.40	
	TOTAL	**£46,717.20**	**£46,717.20**

TASK 11

Sales Day Book

From: 30/04/2016
To: 31/05/2016

Toy Shop
Sales Day Book Report

20 Apr 2017
15:33

Type: Sales QE Invoice

Trx No	Type	Date	Name	Invoice Number	Ref	Details	Net	VAT	Total
14	Sales QE Invoice	04/05/2016	Busy Bee Toys		Inv 2021		2,585.00	517.00	3,102.00
15	Sales QE Invoice	04/05/2016	Forming Fun		Inv 2022		500.00	100.00	600.00
16	Sales QE Invoice	06/05/2016	Teddy T's Party		Inv 2023		5,000.00	1,000.00	6,000.00
						TOTAL	£8,085.00	£1,617.00	£9,702.00

TASK 11

Sales Return Day Book

From: 30/04/2016
To: 31/05/2016

Toy Shop
Sales Day Book Report

20 Apr 2017
15:34

Type: Sales QE Credit

Trx No	Type	Date	Name	Invoice Number	Ref	Details	Net	VAT	Total
17	Sales QE Credit	13/05/2016	Teddy T's Party		CN101	Return faulty computer games	-320.00	-64.00	-384.00
						TOTAL	-£320.00	-£64.00	-£384.00

TASK 11

Purchase Day Book

From: 30/04/2016
To: 31/05/2016

Toy Shop
Purchase Day Book Report

20 Apr 2017
15:36

Type: Purchase QE Invoice

Trx No	Type	Date	Name	Invoice Number	Ref	Details	Net	VAT	Total
18	Purchase QE Invoice	03/05/2016	Abacus C & C		B/989		450.00	90.00	540.00
19	Purchase QE Invoice	05/05/2016	Compugames Ltd		145215		500.00	100.00	600.00
20	Purchase QE Invoice	10/05/2016	Space Models		C-32632		1,000.00	200.00	1,200.00
34	Purchase QE Invoice	10/05/2016	Toys Unlimited		12421		18.00	0.00	18.00
						TOTAL	£1,968.00	£390.00	£2,358.00

TASK 11

Customer Activity Report

Busy Bee Toys (BB01)

Date	Number	Reference	Type	Net	VAT	Total	Discount	Outstanding
30/04/2016		Inv 021	Customer OB Invoice	349.20	0.00	349.20		0.00
04/05/2016		Inv 2021	Sales QE Invoice	2,585.00	517.00	3,102.00		3,102.00
17/05/2016		Chq no 100322	Customer Receipt			-349.20	0.00	0.00
						3,102.00		3,102.00

Forming Fun (FF02)

Date	Number	Reference	Type	Net	VAT	Total	Discount	Outstanding
30/04/2016		Inv 035	Customer OB Invoice	99.60	0.00	99.60		0.00
04/05/2016		Inv 2022	Sales QE Invoice	500.00	100.00	600.00		600.00
17/05/2016		Chq no 267543	Customer Receipt			-99.60	0.00	0.00
						600.00		600.00

Space Models (SM03)

Date	Number	Reference	Type	Net	VAT	Total	Discount	Outstanding
30/04/2016		Inv 093	Customer OB Invoice	1,195.20	0.00	1,195.20		1,195.20
						1,195.20		1,195.20

Teddy T's Party (TP04)

Date	Number	Reference	Type	Net	VAT	Total	Discount	Outstanding
30/04/2016		Inv 1003	Customer OB Invoice	579.60	0.00	579.60		0.00
06/05/2016		Inv 2023	Sales QE Invoice	5,000.00	1,000.00	6,000.00		6,000.00
13/05/2016		CN101	Sales QE Credit	-320.00	-64.00	-384.00		0.00
26/05/2016		BACS	Customer Receipt			-195.60	0.00	0.00
						6,000.00		6,000.00

TASK 11

Supplier Activity Report

From: 30/04/2016
To: 31/05/2016

Toy Shop
Supplier Activity Report

20 Apr 2017
15:39

Abacus C & C (PL01)

Date	Number	Reference	Type	Net	VAT	Total	Discount	Outstanding
30/04/2016		Inv B/1874	Supplier OB Invoice	369.60	0.00	369.60		0.00
03/05/2016		B/989	Purchase QE Invoice	450.00	90.00	540.00		540.00
22/05/2016		Chq no 101333	Supplier Payment			-369.60	0.00	0.00
						540.00		540.00

Compugames Ltd (PL02)

Date	Number	Reference	Type	Net	VAT	Total	Discount	Outstanding
30/04/2016		Inv 1087	Supplier OB Invoice	511.20	0.00	511.20		0.00
05/05/2016		145215	Purchase QE Invoice	500.00	100.00	600.00		0.00
15/05/2016		CR 11245	Purchase QE Credit	-88.00	-17.60	-105.60		0.00
22/05/2016		Chq no 101334	Supplier Payment			-1,005.60	0.00	0.00
						0.00		0.00

Space Models (PL03)

Date	Number	Reference	Type	Net	VAT	Total	Discount	Outstanding
30/04/2016		Inv F-0193	Supplier OB Invoice	306.00	0.00	306.00		306.00
10/05/2016		C-32632	Purchase QE Invoice	1,000.00	200.00	1,200.00		1,200.00
						1,506.00		1,506.00

Toys Unlimited (PL04)

Date	Number	Reference	Type	Net	VAT	Total	Discount	Outstanding
30/04/2016		Inv W/032	Supplier OB Invoice	970.80	0.00	970.80		970.80
10/05/2016		12421	Purchase QE Invoice	18.00	0.00	18.00		18.00
						988.80		988.80

TASK 11

Aged Creditors Report

<table>
<tr><td></td><td></td><td colspan="2" align="center">Toy Shop</td><td colspan="5" align="right">20 Apr 2017</td></tr>
<tr><td colspan="2">To: 31/05/2016</td><td colspan="2" align="center">**Aged Creditors Breakdown**</td><td colspan="5" align="right">15:42</td></tr>
</table>

Date	Reference	Total	Due Date	O/S Amt	< 30 days	< 60 days	< 90 days	Older
Abacus C & C (PL01), Credit limit: £5,500.00								
, Terms: 30 days - OVERDUE								
03/05/2016	B/989	540.00	02/06/2016	540.00	540.00			
				£540.00	£540.00	£0.00	£0.00	£0.00
Space Models (PL03), Credit limit: £2,000.00								
, Terms: 30 days - OVERDUE								
10/05/2016	C-32632	1,200.00	09/06/2016	1,200.00	1,200.00			
30/04/2016	Inv F-0193	306.00	30/05/2016	306.00		306.00		
				£1,506.00	£1,200.00	£306.00	£0.00	£0.00
Toys Unlimited (PL04), Credit limit: £2,000.00								
, Terms: 30 days - OVERDUE								
10/05/2016	12421	18.00	09/06/2016	18.00	18.00			
30/04/2016	Inv W/032	970.80	30/05/2016	970.80		970.80		
				£988.80	£18.00	£970.80	£0.00	£0.00
			TOTAL	£3,034.80	£1,758.00	£1,276.80	£0.00	£0.00

TASK 11

Aged Debtors Report

Toy Shop
Aged Debtors Breakdown

20 Apr 2017
15:43

Date	Reference	Total	Due Date	O/S Amt	< 30 days	< 60 days	< 90 days	Older
Busy Bee Toys (BB01), Credit limit: £4,000.00								
, Terms: 30 days - OVERDUE								
04/05/2016	QE-Inv 2021	3,102.00	03/06/2016	3,102.00	3,102.00			
				£3,102.00	£3,102.00	£0.00	£0.00	£0.00
Forming Fun (FF02), Credit limit: £4,000.00								
, Terms: 30 days - OVERDUE								
04/05/2016	QE-Inv 2022	600.00	03/06/2016	600.00	600.00			
				£600.00	£600.00	£0.00	£0.00	£0.00
Space Models (SM03), Credit limit: £3,000.00								
, Terms: 30 days - OVERDUE								
30/04/2016	OB-Inv 093	1,195.20	30/05/2016	1,195.20		1,195.20		
				£1,195.20	£0.00	£1,195.20	£0.00	£0.00
Teddy T's Party (TP04), Credit limit: £7,000.00								
, Terms: 30 days - OVERDUE								
06/05/2016	QE-Inv 2023	6,000.00	05/06/2016	6,000.00	6,000.00			
				£6,000.00	£6,000.00	£0.00	£0.00	£0.00
			TOTAL	£10,897.20	£9,702.00	£1,195.20	£0.00	£0.00

TASK 12

Customer address screen shot

Forming Fun (Customer) ⊙ ✏
Ref: FF02

OUTSTANDING [1]	OVERDUE [1]	SALES TO DATE [2]	SALES THIS YEAR [0]
£600.00	£600.00	£699.60	£0.00

CREDIT LIMIT	CREDIT TERMS	LAST SALE	AVERAGE SALE
£4,000.00	30 Days	04 May 2016	£349.80

👤 Main Contact
📍 100 Aventi Way, St Albans, AL2 4PM

| Activity | Contacts and Addresses | Payment Details | Options | Notes |

Invoice Address MAIN ✏
Sales

100 Aventi Way
St Albans
Hertfordshire
AL2 4PM
United Kingdom (GB)

Main Contact MAIN ✏

New Contact +

TASK 14

Remittance Advices

Remittance Advice

Date Paid: 28/05/2016

Reference: PL03

Space Models
13 Central Street
Perth
Scotland

Toy Shop
64 Long Lane
Langhorne
North Yorkshire
YO21 3EJ
United Kingdom

Telephone: 01234 567891

VAT Number: GB 123456789

Reference: Chq no 101335

Our Ref	Your Ref	Date	Total Amount	Amount Paid
Inv F-0193		30/04/2016	306.00	306.00
			Total Paid:	**£ 306.00 GBP**

TASK 14

Remittance Advices

Remittance Advice

Date Paid: 28/05/2016

Reference: PL04

Toys Unlimited
95 Cuscaden Road
Edinburgh
Scotland

Toy Shop
64 Long Lane
Langhorne
North Yorkshire
YO21 3EJ
United Kingdom

Telephone: 01234 567891

VAT Number: GB 123456789

Reference: Chq no 101336

Our Ref	Your Ref	Date	Total Amount	Amount Paid
Inv W/032		30/04/2016	970.80	450.00
			Total Paid:	**£ 450.00 GBP**

TASK 14

Remittance Advices

Remittance Advice

Date Paid: 28/05/2016

Reference: PL01

Abacus C & C
Unit 31
Kitts Industrial Estate
St Helens
Lancs

Toy Shop
64 Long Lane
Langhorne
North Yorkshire
YO21 3EJ
United Kingdom

Telephone: 01234 567891

VAT Number: GB 123456789

Reference: BACS

Our Ref	Your Ref	Date	Total Amount	Amount Paid
B/989		03/05/2016	540.00	540.00
			Total Paid:	**£ 540.00 GBP**

TASK 18

Recurring payment

TASK 22

Customer Activity (detailed) Report

From: 30/04/2016
To: 31/05/2016

Toy Shop
Customer Activity Report

21 Apr 2017
10:53

Busy Bee Toys (BB01)

Date	Number	Reference	Type	Net	VAT	Total	Discount	Outstanding
30/04/2016		Inv 021	Customer OB Invoice	349.20	0.00	349.20		0.00
04/05/2016		Inv 2021	Sales QE Invoice	2,585.00	517.00	3,102.00		0.00
17/05/2016		Chq no 100322	Customer Receipt			-349.20	0.00	0.00
29/05/2016			Customer Receipt			-3,102.00	0.00	0.00
						0.00		0.00

Forming Fun (FF02)

Date	Number	Reference	Type	Net	VAT	Total	Discount	Outstanding
30/04/2016		Inv 035	Customer OB Invoice	99.60	0.00	99.60		0.00
04/05/2016		Inv 2022	Sales QE Invoice	500.00	100.00	600.00		200.00
17/05/2016		Chq no 267543	Customer Receipt			-99.60	0.00	0.00
29/05/2016		Chq no 828100	Customer Receipt			-400.00	0.00	0.00
						200.00		200.00

Space Models (SM03)

Date	Number	Reference	Type	Net	VAT	Total	Discount	Outstanding
30/04/2016		Inv 093	Customer OB Invoice	1,195.20	0.00	1,195.20		1,195.20
						1,195.20		1,195.20

Teddy T's Party (TP04)

Date	Number	Reference	Type	Net	VAT	Total	Discount	Outstanding
30/04/2016		Inv 1003	Customer OB Invoice	579.60	0.00	579.60		0.00
06/05/2016		Inv 2023	Sales QE Invoice	5,000.00	1,000.00	6,000.00		0.00
13/05/2016		CN101	Sales QE Credit	-320.00	-64.00	-384.00		0.00
26/05/2016		BACS	Customer Receipt			-195.60	0.00	0.00
29/05/2016		Chq no 672522	Customer Receipt			-6,000.00	0.00	0.00
						0.00		0.00

TASK 22

Supplier Activity (detailed) Report

Toy Shop
Supplier Activity Report

Abacus C & C (PL01)

Date	Number	Reference	Type	Net	VAT	Total	Discount	Outstanding
30/04/2016		Inv B/1874	Supplier OB Invoice	369.60	0.00	369.60		0.00
03/05/2016		B/989	Purchase QE Invoice	450.00	90.00	540.00		0.00
22/05/2016		Chq no 101333	Supplier Payment			-369.60	0.00	0.00
28/05/2016		BACS	Supplier Payment			-540.00	0.00	0.00
						0.00		0.00

Compugames Ltd (PL02)

Date	Number	Reference	Type	Net	VAT	Total	Discount	Outstanding
30/04/2016		Inv 1087	Supplier OB Invoice	511.20	0.00	511.20		0.00
05/05/2016		145215	Purchase QE Invoice	500.00	100.00	600.00		0.00
15/05/2016		CR 11245	Purchase QE Credit	-88.00	-17.60	-105.60		0.00
22/05/2016		Chq no 101334	Supplier Payment			-1,005.60	0.00	0.00
						0.00		0.00

Space Models (PL03)

Date	Number	Reference	Type	Net	VAT	Total	Discount	Outstanding
30/04/2016		Inv F-0193	Supplier OB Invoice	306.00	0.00	306.00		0.00
10/05/2016		C-32632	Purchase QE Invoice	1,000.00	200.00	1,200.00		1,200.00
28/05/2016		Chq no 101335	Supplier Payment			-306.00	0.00	0.00
						1,200.00		1,200.00

Toys Unlimited (PL04)

Date	Number	Reference	Type	Net	VAT	Total	Discount	Outstanding
30/04/2016		Inv W/032	Supplier OB Invoice	970.80	0.00	970.80		520.80
10/05/2016		12421	Purchase QE Invoice	18.00	0.00	18.00		18.00
28/05/2016		Chq no 101336	Supplier Payment			-450.00	0.00	0.00
						538.80		538.80

TASK 22

Period Trial Balance for May

Toy Shop
Trial Balance Report

21 Apr 2017
11:05

This period only

Nominal Code	Name	Debit	Credit
0040	Fixtures and fittings - Cost	5,800.00	
0050	Motor Vehicles - Cost	3,000.00	
1100	Trade Debtors	1,395.20	
1200	Current	24,337.80	
1210	Cash	300.00	
1220	Deposit	500.00	
2100	Trade Creditors		1,738.80
2200	VAT on Sales		2,819.90
2201	VAT on Purchases	483.48	
2500	Loan		10,000.00
3200	Capital introduced		20,000.00
3260	Drawings - equity	2,355.00	
4000	Sales - Computer Games		15,560.00
4001	Sales - Jigsaws		3,144.50
4002	Sales - Boxed Games		2,467.00
5000	Purchases - Computer Games	9,362.00	
5001	Purchases - Jigsaws	3,218.00	
5002	Purchases - Boxed Games	2,965.00	
7100	Rent and rates	1,048.00	
7200	Electricity	669.00	
7500	Office Stationery	53.00	
7610	Insurance	100.00	
7900	Bank charges and interest	101.32	
8201	Subscriptions	32.00	
8205	Refreshments	10.40	
	TOTAL	£55,730.20	£55,730.20

TASK 22

Audit Trail for May (detailed – transactions only including bank reconciled)

From: 30/04/2016
To: 31/05/2016

Toy Shop
Audit Trail Breakdown

21 Apr 2017
11:06

Type: All, Status: All

Trx No	Entry Date	User	Trx Date	Name	Type	Invoice Number	Ref	Ledger Account	Debit	Credit	Bank Reconciled
1	20/04/2017	LH	30/04/2016	Busy Bee Toys (BB01)	Customer OB Invoice		Inv 021	Opening Balances Control Account (9998)		349.20	No
								Trade Debtors (1100)	349.20		No
2	20/04/2017	LH	30/04/2016	Forming Fun (FF02)	Customer OB Invoice		Inv 035	Opening Balances Control Account (9998)		99.60	No
								Trade Debtors (1100)	99.60		No
3	20/04/2017	LH	30/04/2016	Space Models (SM03)	Customer OB Invoice		Inv 093	Opening Balances Control Account (9998)		1,195.20	No
								Trade Debtors (1100)	1,195.20		No
4	20/04/2017	LH	30/04/2016	Teddy T's Party (TP04)	Customer OB Invoice		Inv 1003	Opening Balances Control Account (9998)		579.60	No
								Trade Debtors (1100)	579.60		No
5	20/04/2017	LH	30/04/2016	Abacus C & C (PL01)	Supplier OB Invoice		Inv B/1874	Trade Creditors (2100)		369.60	No
								Opening Balances Control Account (9998)	369.60		No
6	20/04/2017	LH	30/04/2016	Compugames Ltd (PL02)	Supplier OB Invoice		Inv 1087	Trade Creditors (2100)		511.20	No
								Opening Balances Control Account (9998)	511.20		No
7	20/04/2017	LH	30/04/2016	Space Models (PL03)	Supplier OB Invoice		Inv F-0193	Trade Creditors (2100)		306.00	No
								Opening Balances Control Account (9998)	306.00		No
8	20/04/2017	LH	30/04/2016	Toys Unlimited (PL04)	Supplier OB Invoice		Inv W/032	Trade Creditors (2100)		970.80	No
								Opening Balances Control Account (9998)	970.80		No
9	20/04/2017	LH	30/04/2016		Bank Opening Balance			Opening Balances Control Account (9998)		4,225.00	No
								Current (1200)	4,225.00		Yes
10	20/04/2017	LH	30/04/2016		Bank Opening Balance			Opening Balances Control Account (9998)		300.00	No
								Cash (1210)	300.00		No
12	20/04/2017	LH	30/04/2016		Journal Opening Balance		OB 1/5/16	VAT on Sales (2200)		543.00	No
								Opening Balances Control Account (9998)	543.00		No

From: 30/04/2016
To: 31/05/2016

Toy Shop
Audit Trail Breakdown

21 Apr 2017
11:06

								Ledger Account	Debit	Credit	Bank Reconciled
								VAT on Purchases (2201)	109.00		No
								Opening Balances Control Account (9998)		109.00	No
								Capital introduced (3200)		20,000.00	No
								Opening Balances Control Account (9998)	20,000.00		No
								Drawings - equity (3260)	355.00		No
								Opening Balances Control Account (9998)		355.00	No
								Sales - Computer Games (4000)		6,080.00	No
								Opening Balances Control Account (9998)	6,080.00		No
								Sales - Jigsaws (4001)		700.00	No
								Opening Balances Control Account (9998)	700.00		No
								Sales - Boxed Games (4002)		1,967.00	No
								Opening Balances Control Account (9998)	1,967.00		No
								Purchases - Computer Games (5000)	8,000.00		No
								Opening Balances Control Account (9998)		8,000.00	No
								Purchases - Jigsaws (5001)	3,200.00		No
								Opening Balances Control Account (9998)		3,200.00	No
								Purchases - Boxed Games (5002)	2,465.00		No
								Opening Balances Control Account (9998)		2,465.00	No
								Office Stationery (7500)	53.00		No
								Opening Balances Control Account (9998)		53.00	No
								Electricity (7200)	167.00		No
								Opening Balances Control Account (9998)		167.00	No
								Rent and rates (7100)	1,550.00		No
								Opening Balances Control Account (9998)		1,550.00	No
								Fixtures and fittings - Cost (0040)	5,800.00		No
								Opening Balances Control Account (9998)		5,800.00	No

							Account	Debit	Credit	Rec
							Motor Vehicles – Cost (0050)	3,000.00		No
							Opening Balances Control Account (9998)		3,000.00	No
13	20/04/2017	LH	01/05/2016		Bank Transfer	TRANS01	Current (1200)		500.00	Yes
							Deposit (1220)	500.00		No
14	20/04/2017	LH	04/05/2016	Busy Bee Toys (BB01)	Sales QE Invoice	Inv 2021	Sales – Computer Games (4000)		2,585.00	No
							VAT on Sales (2200)		517.00	No
							Trade Debtors (1100)	3,102.00		No
15	20/04/2017	LH	04/05/2016	Forming Fun (FF02)	Sales QE Invoice	Inv 2022	Sales – Boxed Games (4002)		500.00	No
							VAT on Sales (2200)		100.00	No
							Trade Debtors (1100)	600.00		No
16	20/04/2017	LH	06/05/2016	Teddy T's Party (TP04)	Sales QE Invoice	Inv 2023	Sales – Computer Games (4000)		5,000.00	No
							VAT on Sales (2200)		1,000.00	No
							Trade Debtors (1100)	6,000.00		No
17	20/04/2017	LH	13/05/2016	Teddy T's Party (TP04)	Sales QE Credit	CN101	Trade Debtors (1100)		384.00	No
							Sales – Computer Games (4000)	320.00		No
							VAT on Sales (2200)	64.00		No
18	20/04/2017	LH	03/05/2016	Abacus C & C (PL01)	Purchase QE Invoice	B/989	Trade Creditors (2100)		540.00	No
							Purchases – Computer Games (5000)	450.00		No
							VAT on Purchases (2201)	90.00		No
19	20/04/2017	LH	05/05/2016	Compugames Ltd (PL02)	Purchase QE Invoice	145215	Trade Creditors (2100)		600.00	No
							Purchases – Boxed Games (5002)	500.00		No
							VAT on Purchases (2201)	100.00		No
20	20/04/2017	LH	10/05/2016	Space Models (PL03)	Purchase QE Invoice	C-32632	Trade Creditors (2100)		1,200.00	No
							Purchases – Computer Games (5000)	1,000.00		No
							VAT on Purchases (2201)	200.00		No
22	20/04/2017	LH	15/05/2016	Compugames Ltd (PL02)	Purchase QE Credit	CR 11245	Purchases – Computer Games (5000)		88.00	No
							VAT on Purchases (2201)		17.60	No
							Trade Creditors (2100)	105.60		No
23	20/04/2017	LH	17/05/2016	Busy Bee Toys (BB01)	Customer Receipt	Chq no 100322	Trade Debtors (1100)		349.20	No
							Current (1200)	349.20		Yes
24	20/04/2017	LH	17/05/2016	Forming Fun (FF02)	Customer Receipt	Chq no 267543	Trade Debtors (1100)		99.60	No
							Current (1200)	99.60		Yes
25	20/04/2017	LH	26/05/2016	Teddy T's Party (TP04)	Customer Receipt	BACS	Trade Debtors (1100)		579.60	No
							Trade Debtors (1100)	384.00		No
							Current (1200)	195.60		Yes
26	20/04/2017	LH	22/05/2016	Abacus C & C (PL01)	Supplier Payment	Chq no 101333	Trade Creditors (2100)	369.60		No
							Current (1200)		369.60	Yes
27	20/04/2017	LH	22/05/2016	Compugames Ltd (PL02)	Supplier Payment	Chq no 101334	Trade Creditors (2100)	511.20		No
							Trade Creditors (2100)	600.00		No
							Trade Creditors (2100)		105.60	No
							Current (1200)		1,005.60	Yes
28	20/04/2017	LH	13/05/2016		Other Receipt	Cash sale	Sales – Computer Games (4000)		1,000.00	No
							VAT on Sales (2200)		200.00	No
							Current (1200)	1,200.00		Yes
29	20/04/2017	LH	13/05/2016		Other Receipt	Cash sale	Sales – Jigsaws (4001)		2,399.50	No
							VAT on Sales (2200)		479.90	No
							Current (1200)	2,879.40		Yes
30	20/04/2017	LH	20/05/2016		Other Receipt	Cash sale	Sales – Computer Games (4000)		995.00	No
							Current (1200)	995.00		Yes
31	20/04/2017	LH	20/05/2016		Other Payment	Voucher 012	Cash (1210)		32.00	No
							Subscriptions (8201)	32.00		No
32	20/04/2017	LH	21/05/2016		Other Payment	Voucher 013	Cash (1210)		12.48	No
							Refreshments (8205)	10.40		No
							VAT on Purchases (2201)	2.08		No

33	20/04/2017	LH	25/05/2016		Journal	JNL02	Drawings - equity (3260)	2,000.00		No
							Current (1200)		2,000.00	Yes
34	20/04/2017	LH	10/05/2016	Toys Unlimited (PL04)	Purchase QE Invoice	12421	Trade Creditors (2100)		18.00	No
							Purchases - Jigsaws (5001)	18.00		No
35	20/04/2017	LH	31/05/2016		Journal	JNL03	Electricity (7200)	502.00		No
							Rent and rates (7100)		502.00	No
36	20/04/2017	LH	28/05/2016	Space Models (PL03)	Supplier Payment	Chq no 101335	Trade Creditors (2100)	306.00		No
							Current (1200)		306.00	No
37	20/04/2017	LH	28/05/2016	Toys Unlimited (PL04)	Supplier Payment	Chq no 101336	Trade Creditors (2100)	450.00		No
							Current (1200)		450.00	Yes
38	20/04/2017	LH	28/05/2016	Abacus C & C (PL01)	Supplier Payment	BACS	Trade Creditors (2100)	540.00		No
							Current (1200)		540.00	Yes
39	20/04/2017	LH	29/05/2016	Busy Bee Toys (BB01)	Customer Receipt		Trade Debtors (1100)		3,102.00	No
							Current (1200)	3,102.00		Yes
40	20/04/2017	LH	29/05/2016	Forming Fun (FF02)	Customer Receipt	Chq no 828100	Trade Debtors (1100)		400.00	No
							Current (1200)	400.00		Yes
41	20/04/2017	LH	29/05/2016	Teddy T's Party (TP04)	Customer Receipt	Chq no 672522	Trade Debtors (1100)		6,000.00	No
							Current (1200)	6,000.00		Yes
42	20/04/2017	LH	14/05/2016		Other Receipt	CSH41	Sales - Computer Games (4000)		220.00	No
							VAT on Sales (2200)		44.00	No
							Current (1200)	264.00		Yes
43	20/04/2017	LH	19/05/2016		Other Receipt	Debit card	Sales - Jigsaws (4001)		45.00	No
							VAT on Sales (2200)			No
							Current (1200)	45.00		Yes
46	20/04/2017	LH	31/05/2016		Other Payment	Direct Debit Insurance	Current (1200)		100.00	Yes
							Insurance (7610)	100.00		No
							VAT on Purchases (2201)			No
57	20/04/2017	LH	31/05/2016		Journal	JNL04	Current (1200)	10,000.00		Yes
							Loan (2500)		10,000.00	No
58	21/04/2017	LH	31/05/2016		Bank Transfer	CSH25	Current (1200)		44.48	Yes
							Cash (1210)	44.48		No
59	21/04/2017	LH	31/05/2016		Bank Payment	Bank Charge	Current (1200)		101.32	Yes
							Bank charges and interest (7900)	101.32		No

TASK 22

Aged Debtors (summary)

Customer	Credit limit	O/S Amt	< 30 days	< 60 days	< 90 days	Older
To: 31/05/2016 — Toy Shop — Aged Debtors Report — 21 Apr 2017 11:16						
Forming Fun (FF02)	£4,000.00	£200.00	£200.00	£0.00	£0.00	£0.00
Space Models (SM03)	£3,000.00	£1,195.20	£0.00	£1,195.20	£0.00	£0.00
TOTAL		£1,395.20	£200.00	£1,195.20	£0.00	£0.00

PRACTICE PAPER 2

CRAZY HAIR ANSWERS

TASK 3.2

Customer Address List

		Crazy Hair			21 Apr 2017	
		Customer Address List			12:06	

Address Types: All

Customer Name	Address	Contact name	Phone	Mobile	Email	Fax
Alfred Images (104)	Masuki Offices PO Box 5684 Birmingham B23 4RD	Main Contact				
Figgaro (110)	Beta Studio 34 Knightsbridge Way Morden SE23 4KA	Main Contact				
Blades (118)	Alpha Studio 45 Key West London SE1 0JF	Main Contact				
Hair Studio (122)	Framlington Court Lee London SE4 7YH	Main Contact				
Ribbons & Curls (138)	PO Box 1120 Canning Town London TN2 2EB	Main Contact				

TASK 3.2

Supplier Address List

		Crazy Hair			21 Apr 2017	
		Supplier Address List			12:12	

Address Types: All

Supplier Name	Address	Contact name	Phone	Mobile	Email	Fax
Avada Cash & Carry (1134)	32 Surrey Quay Isle of Dogs E12 3NW	Main Contact				
Straightside Supplies (1138)	Havering Place Holbom London WC1 2PP	Main Contact				
Hair Supplies (1165)	43 St Helens Way London SE7 3RF	Main Contact				
Wig Specialists (1185)	Retro Square 32 Wigmore Road London EC1V 3SG	Main Contact				

TASK 3.2

Trial Balance

From: 30/04/2016
To: 31/05/2016

Crazy Hair
Trial Balance Report

21 Apr 2017
12:18

This period only

Nominal Code	Name	Selected Period	
		Debit	Credit
0040	Fixtures and fittings - Cost	31,000.00	
0050	Motor Vehicles - Cost	24,000.00	
1100	Trade Debtors	8,907.60	
1200	Current	54,210.81	
1210	Petty Cash	200.00	
2100	Trade Creditors		7,214.40
2200	VAT on Sales		5,550.00
2201	VAT on Purchases	1,507.94	
3200	Capital introduced		165,000.00
3260	Drawings - equity	5,000.00	
4000	Sales - Brushes		345.00
4001	Sales - Combs		187.00
4002	Sales - Colours		3,801.45
4003	Sales - Hairdryers		758.00
4004	Sales - Wigs		5,600.00
4005	Cash Sales		617.50
5000	Purchases - Brushes	873.00	
5001	Purchases - Combs	50.00	
5002	Purchases - Colour	4,200.00	
5003	Purchases - Hairdryers	6,310.00	
5004	Purchases - Wigs	52,814.00	
	TOTAL	£189,073.35	£189,073.35

KAPLAN PUBLISHING

TASK 9

Remittance advices

Remittance Advice

Date Paid: 31/05/2016

Reference: 1185

Wigs Specialist
Retro Square
32 Wigmore Road
London
EC1V 3SG

Crazy Hair
34 Clapham Road
Clapham
London
SE3 2HR
United Kingdom

Telephone: 01234 567891

VAT Number: GB 123456789

Reference: Chq no 163455

Our Ref	Your Ref	Date	Total Amount	Amount Paid
Inv S653		30/04/2016	102.00	102.00
			Total Paid:	**£ 102.00 GBP**

Remittance Advice

Date Paid: 31/05/2016

Reference: 1134

Avada Cash & Carry
32 Surrey Quay
Isle of Dogs
E12 3NW

Crazy Hair
34 Clapham Road
Clapham
London
SE3 2HR
United Kingdom

Telephone: 01234 567891

VAT Number: GB 123456789

Reference: Chq No 163456

Our Ref	Your Ref	Date	Total Amount	Amount Paid
Inv C/251		30/04/2016	4,454.40	4,454.40
			Total Paid:	**£ 4,454.40 GBP**

Remittance Advice

Date Paid: 31/05/2016

Reference: 1165

Hair Supplies
43 St Helens Way
London
SE7 3RF

Crazy Hair
34 Clapham Road
Clapham
London
SE3 2HR
United Kingdom

Telephone: 01234 567891

VAT Number: GB 123456789

Reference: Chq no 163457

Our Ref	Your Ref	Date	Total Amount	Amount Paid
Inv 0028		30/04/2016	818.40	818.40
			Total Paid:	**£ 818.40 GBP**

TASK 12

Trial Balance

From: 30/04/2016
To: 31/05/2016

Crazy Hair
Trial Balance Report

24 Apr 2017
13:32

This period only

Nominal Code	Name	Selected Period	
		Debit	Credit
0040	Fixtures and fittings - Cost	31,000.00	
0050	Motor Vehicles - Cost	24,000.00	
1100	Trade Debtors	5,964.33	
1200	Current	57,373.41	
1210	Petty Cash	155.17	
2100	Trade Creditors		7,341.96
2200	VAT on Sales		6,482.35
2201	VAT on Purchases	2,401.96	
3200	Capital introduced		165,000.00
3260	Drawings - equity	5,000.00	
4000	Sales - Brushes		1,204.30
4001	Sales - Combs		187.00
4002	Sales - Colours		4,172.85
4003	Sales - Hairdryers		1,621.40
4004	Sales - Wigs		8,167.68
4005	Cash Sales		617.50
5000	Purchases - Brushes	1,064.60	
5001	Purchases - Combs	50.00	
5002	Purchases - Colour	5,154.00	
5003	Purchases - Hairdryers	6,488.56	
5004	Purchases - Wigs	56,104.90	
7400	Travel and Entertainment	33.60	
7500	Office costs	4.51	
	TOTAL	£194,795.04	£194,795.04

TASK 12

Sales Day Book

From: 30/04/2016
To: 31/05/2016

Crazy Hair
Sales Day Book Report

24 Apr 2017
13:34

Type: Sales QE Invoice

Trx No	Type	Date	Name	Invoice Number	Ref	Details	Net	VAT	Total
13	Sales QE Invoice	12/05/2016	Ribbons & Curls		Inv 3353		141.00	28.20	169.20
14	Sales QE Invoice	12/05/2016	Alfred Images		Inv 3354		581.00	116.20	697.20
15	Sales QE Invoice	13/05/2016	Figgaro		Inv 3355		660.00	132.00	792.00
16	Sales QE Invoice	15/05/2016	Blades		Inv 3356		1,685.76	337.15	2,022.91
17	Sales QE Invoice	15/05/2016	Blades		Inv 3356		203.40	40.68	244.08
18	Sales QE Invoice	18/05/2016	Hair Studio		Inv 3357		316.80	63.36	380.16
19	Sales QE Invoice	18/05/2016	Hair Studio		Inv 3357		881.92	176.38	1,058.30
20	Sales QE Invoice	18/05/2016	Hair Studio		Inv 3357		230.40	46.08	276.48
						TOTAL	£4,700.28	£940.05	£5,640.33

TASK 12

Sales Returns Day Book

From: 30/04/2016
To: 31/05/2016

Crazy Hair
Sales Day Book Report

24 Apr 2017
13:35

Type: Sales QE Credit

Trx No	Type	Date	Name	Invoice Number	Ref	Details	Net	VAT	Total
21	Sales QE Credit	25/05/2016	Alfred Images		CN23		-56.00	-11.20	-67.20
						TOTAL	-£56.00	-£11.20	-£67.20

TASK 12

Purchase Day Book

				Crazy Hair						

From: 30/04/2016
To: 31/05/2016

Crazy Hair
Purchase Day Book Report

24 Apr 2017
13:36

Type: Purchase QE Invoice

Trx No	Type	Date	Name	Invoice Number	Ref	Details	Net	VAT	Total
22	Purchase QE Invoice	11/05/2016	Straightside Supplies		Inv 3362		191.60	38.32	229.92
37	Purchase QE Invoice	11/05/2016	Avada Cash & Carry		Inv C/910		954.00	190.80	1,144.80
24	Purchase QE Invoice	13/05/2016	Hair Supplies		Inv 0814		178.56	0.00	178.56
25	Purchase QE Invoice	14/05/2016	Wig Specialists		Inv S1198		3,393.60	678.72	4,072.32
						TOTAL	£4,717.76	£907.84	£5,625.60

TASK 12

Customer Activity Report

From: 30/04/2016
To: 31/05/2016

Crazy Hair
Customer Activity Report

24 Apr 2017
13:38

Alfred Images (104)

Date	Number	Reference	Type	Net	VAT	Total	Discount	Outstanding
30/04/2016		Inv 3352	Customer OB Invoice	1,809.60	0.00	1,809.60		0.00
12/05/2016		Inv 3354	Sales QE Invoice	581.00	116.20	697.20		697.20
20/05/2016		Cheque no 183001	Customer Receipt			-1,809.60	0.00	0.00
25/05/2016		CN23	Sales QE Credit	-56.00	-11.20	-67.20		-67.20
						630.00		630.00

Figgaro (110)

Date	Number	Reference	Type	Net	VAT	Total	Discount	Outstanding
30/04/2016		Inv 2856	Customer OB Invoice	3,880.80	0.00	3,880.80		0.00
13/05/2016		Inv 3355	Sales QE Invoice	660.00	132.00	792.00		792.00
21/05/2016		BACS	Customer Receipt			-3,880.80	0.00	0.00
						792.00		792.00

Blades (118)

Date	Number	Reference	Type	Net	VAT	Total	Discount	Outstanding
30/04/2016		Inv 3345	Customer OB Invoice	2,144.40	0.00	2,144.40		0.00
15/05/2016		Inv 3356	Sales QE Invoice	1,685.76	337.15	2,022.91		2,022.91
15/05/2016		Inv 3356	Sales QE Invoice	203.40	40.68	244.08		244.08
21/05/2016		Chq no 654255	Customer Receipt			-2,144.40	0.00	0.00
						2,266.99		2,266.99

TASK 12

Customer Activity Report (continued)

Hair Studio (122)

Date	Number	Reference	Type	Net	VAT	Total	Discount	Outstanding
30/04/2016		Inv 3098	Customer OB Invoice	681.60	0.00	681.60		0.00
18/05/2016		Inv 3357	Sales QE Invoice	316.80	63.36	380.16		380.16
18/05/2016		Inv 3357	Sales QE Invoice	881.92	176.38	1,058.30		1,058.30
18/05/2016		Inv 3357	Sales QE Invoice	230.40	46.08	276.48		276.48
21/05/2016		Chq no 452221	Customer Receipt			-681.60	0.00	0.00
						1,714.94		1,714.94

Who: Leanne Halsall   Produced by Sage One   Page 1 of 2

From: 30/04/2016
To: 31/05/2016

Crazy Hair
Customer Activity Report

24 Apr 2017
13:38

Ribbons & Curls (138)

Date	Number	Reference	Type	Net	VAT	Total	Discount	Outstanding
30/04/2016		Inv 3123	Customer OB Invoice	391.20	0.00	391.20		391.20
12/05/2016		Inv 3353	Sales QE Invoice	141.00	28.20	169.20		169.20
						560.40		560.40

TASK 12

Supplier Activity Report

Crazy Hair
Supplier Activity Report

24 Apr 2017
13:40

Avada Cash & Carry (1134)

Date	Number	Reference	Type	Net	VAT	Total	Discount	Outstanding
30/04/2016		Inv C/251	Supplier OB Invoice	4,454.40	0.00	4,454.40		0.00
11/05/2016		Inv C/910	Purchase QE Invoice	954.00	190.80	1,144.80		1,144.80
31/05/2016		Chq No 163456	Supplier Payment			-4,454.40	0.00	0.00
						1,144.80		1,144.80

Straightside Supplies (1138)

Date	Number	Reference	Type	Net	VAT	Total	Discount	Outstanding
30/04/2016		Inv 9140	Supplier OB Invoice	1,839.60	0.00	1,839.60		1,839.60
11/05/2016		Inv 3362	Purchase QE Invoice	191.60	38.32	229.92		229.92
						2,069.52		2,069.52

Hair Supplies (1165)

Date	Number	Reference	Type	Net	VAT	Total	Discount	Outstanding
30/04/2016		Inv 0028	Supplier OB Invoice	818.40	0.00	818.40		0.00
13/05/2016		Inv 0814	Purchase QE Invoice	178.56	0.00	178.56		178.56
31/05/2016		Chq no 163457	Supplier Payment			-818.40	0.00	0.00
						178.56		178.56

Wigs Specialist (1185)

Date	Number	Reference	Type	Net	VAT	Total	Discount	Outstanding
30/04/2016		Inv S653	Supplier OB Invoice	102.00	0.00	102.00		0.00
14/05/2016		Inv S1198	Purchase QE Invoice	3,393.60	678.72	4,072.32		4,072.32
18/05/2016		C3223	Purchase QE Credit	-102.70	-20.54	-123.24		-123.24
31/05/2016		Chq no 163455	Supplier Payment			-102.00	0.00	0.00
						3,949.08		3,949.08

TASK 12

Aged Creditors Report (summary)

	Crazy Hair					
To: 31/05/2016	**Aged Creditors Report**				24 Apr 2017	13:42

Supplier	Credit limit	O/S Amt	< 30 days	< 60 days	< 90 days	Older
Avada Cash & Carry (1134)	£5,500.00	£1,144.80	£1,144.80	£0.00	£0.00	£0.00
Hair Supplies (1165)	£4,000.00	£178.56	£178.56	£0.00	£0.00	£0.00
Straightside Supplies (1138)	£12,000.00	£2,069.52	£229.92	£1,839.60	£0.00	£0.00
Wigs Specialist (1185)	£5,000.00	£3,949.08	£3,949.08	£0.00	£0.00	£0.00
TOTAL		£7,341.96	£5,502.36	£1,839.60	£0.00	£0.00

TASK 12

Aged Debtors Report (summary)

	Crazy Hair					
To: 31/05/2016	**Aged Debtors Report**				24 Apr 2017	13:43

Customer	Credit limit	O/S Amt	< 30 days	< 60 days	< 90 days	Older
Alfred Images (104)	£8,000.00	£630.00	£630.00	£0.00	£0.00	£0.00
Blades (118)	£6,100.00	£2,266.99	£2,266.99	£0.00	£0.00	£0.00
Figgaro (110)	£6,500.00	£792.00	£792.00	£0.00	£0.00	£0.00
Hair Studio (122)	£5,000.00	£1,714.94	£1,714.94	£0.00	£0.00	£0.00
Ribbons & Curls (138)	£5,000.00	£560.40	£169.20	£391.20	£0.00	£0.00
TOTAL		£5,964.33	£5,573.13	£391.20	£0.00	£0.00

Task 14

Customer change of address

Ribbons & Curls (Customer) ✏

Ref: 138

OUTSTANDING [2]	OVERDUE [2]	SALES TO DATE [2]	SALES THIS YEAR [0]
£560.40	**£560.40**	**£560.40**	**£0.00**

CREDIT LIMIT	CREDIT TERMS	LAST SALE	AVERAGE SALE
£5,000.00	**30 Days**	**12 May 2016**	**£280.20**

Activity	Contacts and Addresses	Payment Details	Options	Notes

Invoice Address [MAIN] ✏

Sales

122 Devonshire Road
Cranbrook
London
SE1 2AB
United Kingdom (GB)

Main Contact [MAIN] ✏

TASK 17

Customer Address List

Crazy Hair
Customer Address List

25 Apr 2017
09:42

Address Types: All

Customer Name	Address	Contact name	Phone	Mobile	Email	Fax
Alfred Images (104)	Masuki Offices PO Box 5684 Birmingham B23 4RD	Main Contact				
Figgaro (110)	Beta Studio 34 Knightsbridge Way Morden SE23 4KA	Main Contact				
Blades (118)	Alpha Studio 45 Key West London SE1 0JF	Main Contact				
Hair Studio (122)	Framlington Court Lee London SE4 7YH	Main Contact				
Ribbons & Curls (138)	122 Devonshire Road Cranbrook London SE1 2AB	Main Contact				

TASK 17

Customer Activity

Alfred Images (104)

Date	Number	Reference	Type	Net	VAT	Total	Discount	Outstanding
30/04/2016		Inv 3352	Customer OB Invoice	1,809.60	0.00	1,809.60		0.00
12/05/2016		Inv 3354	Sales QE Invoice	581.00	116.20	697.20		697.20
20/05/2016		Cheque no 183001	Customer Receipt			-1,809.60	0.00	0.00
25/05/2016		CN23	Sales QE Credit	-56.00	-11.20	-67.20		-67.20
						630.00		630.00

Figgaro (110)

Date	Number	Reference	Type	Net	VAT	Total	Discount	Outstanding
30/04/2016		Inv 2856	Customer OB Invoice	3,880.80	0.00	3,880.80		0.00
13/05/2016		Inv 3355	Sales QE Invoice	660.00	132.00	792.00		792.00
21/05/2016		BACS	Customer Receipt			-3,880.80	0.00	0.00
						792.00		792.00

Blades (118)

Date	Number	Reference	Type	Net	VAT	Total	Discount	Outstanding
30/04/2016		Inv 3345	Customer OB Invoice	2,144.40	0.00	2,144.40		0.00
15/05/2016		Inv 3356	Sales QE Invoice	1,685.76	337.15	2,022.91		2,022.91
15/05/2016		Inv 3356	Sales QE Invoice	203.40	40.68	244.08		244.08
21/05/2016		Chq no 654255	Customer Receipt			-2,144.40	0.00	0.00
						2,266.99		2,266.99

Hair Studio (122)

Date	Number	Reference	Type	Net	VAT	Total	Discount	Outstanding
30/04/2016		Inv 3098	Customer OB Invoice	681.60	0.00	681.60		0.00
18/05/2016		Inv 3357	Sales QE Invoice	316.80	63.36	380.16		380.16
18/05/2016		Inv 3357	Sales QE Invoice	881.92	176.38	1,058.30		1,058.30
18/05/2016		Inv 3357	Sales QE Invoice	230.40	46.08	276.48		276.48
21/05/2016		Chq no 452221	Customer Receipt			-681.60	0.00	0.00
						1,714.94		1,714.94

Ribbons & Curls (138)

Date	Number	Reference	Type	Net	VAT	Total	Discount	Outstanding
30/04/2016		Inv 3123	Customer OB Invoice	391.20	0.00	391.20		391.20
12/05/2016		Inv 3353	Sales QE Invoice	141.00	28.20	169.20		169.20
						560.40		560.40

TASK 17

Supplier Activity

Crazy Hair
Supplier Activity Report

Avada Cash & Carry (1134)

Date	Number	Reference	Type	Net	VAT	Total	Discount	Outstanding
30/04/2016		Inv C/251	Supplier OB Invoice	4,454.40	0.00	4,454.40		0.00
11/05/2016		Inv C/910	Purchase QE Invoice	954.00	190.80	1,144.80		1,144.80
31/05/2016		Chq No 163456	Supplier Payment			-4,454.40	0.00	0.00
						1,144.80		1,144.80

Straightside Supplies (1138)

Date	Number	Reference	Type	Net	VAT	Total	Discount	Outstanding
30/04/2016		Inv 9140	Supplier OB Invoice	1,839.60	0.00	1,839.60		1,839.60
11/05/2016		Inv 3362	Purchase QE Invoice	191.60	38.32	229.92		229.92
						2,069.52		2,069.52

Hair Supplies (1165)

Date	Number	Reference	Type	Net	VAT	Total	Discount	Outstanding
30/04/2016		Inv 0028	Supplier OB Invoice	818.40	0.00	818.40		0.00
13/05/2016		Inv 0814	Purchase QE Invoice	178.56	0.00	178.56		178.56
31/05/2016		Chq no 163457	Supplier Payment			-818.40	0.00	0.00
						178.56		178.56

Wigs Specialist (1185)

Date	Number	Reference	Type	Net	VAT	Total	Discount	Outstanding
30/04/2016		Inv S653	Supplier OB Invoice	102.00	0.00	102.00		0.00
14/05/2016		Inv S1198	Purchase QE Invoice	3,393.60	678.72	4,072.32		4,072.32
18/05/2016		C3223	Purchase QE Credit	-102.70	-20.54	-123.24		-123.24
31/05/2016		Chq no 163455	Supplier Payment			-102.00	0.00	0.00
						3,949.08		3,949.08

TASK 17

Trial Balance for the month of May

From: 30/04/2016
To: 31/05/2016

Crazy Hair
Trial Balance Report

25 Apr 2017
09:53

This period only

Nominal Code	Name	Selected Period	
		Debit	Credit
0040	Fixtures and fittings - Cost	31,000.00	
0050	Motor Vehicles - Cost	24,000.00	
1100	Trade Debtors	5,964.33	
1200	Current	56,640.84	
1210	Petty Cash	185.69	
2100	Trade Creditors		7,341.96
2200	VAT on Sales		6,482.35
2201	VAT on Purchases	2,401.96	
3200	Capital introduced		165,000.00
3260	Drawings - equity	5,440.00	
4000	Sales - Brushes		1,204.30
4001	Sales - Combs		187.00
4002	Sales - Colours		4,172.85
4003	Sales - Hairdryers		1,621.40
4004	Sales - Wigs		8,167.68
4005	Cash Sales		617.50
5000	Purchases - Brushes	1,064.60	
5001	Purchases - Combs	50.00	
5002	Purchases - Colour	5,154.00	
5003	Purchases - Hairdryers	6,488.56	
5004	Purchases - Wigs	56,104.90	
7200	Electricity	66.94	
7400	Travel and Entertainment	33.60	
7500	Office costs	4.51	
7610	Premises Insurance	168.00	
7900	Bank charges and interest	27.11	
	TOTAL	£194,795.04	£194,795.04

TASK 17

Audit Trail for May only (Detailed & include opening balance)

From: 30/04/2016
To: 31/05/2016

Crazy Hair
Audit Trail Breakdown

25 Apr 2017
09:55

Type: All, Status: All

Trx No	Entry Date	User	Trx Date	Name	Type	Invoice Number	Ref	Ledger Account	Debit	Credit	Bank Reconciled
1	21/04/2017	LH	30/04/2016	Alfred Images (104)	Customer OB Invoice		Inv 3352	Opening Balances Control Account (9998)		1,809.60	No
								Trade Debtors (1100)	1,809.60		No
2	21/04/2017	LH	30/04/2016	Figgaro (110)	Customer OB Invoice		Inv 2856	Opening Balances Control Account (9998)		3,880.80	No
								Trade Debtors (1100)	3,880.80		No
3	21/04/2017	LH	30/04/2016	Blades (118)	Customer OB Invoice		Inv 3345	Opening Balances Control Account (9998)		2,144.40	No
								Trade Debtors (1100)	2,144.40		No
4	21/04/2017	LH	30/04/2016	Hair Studio (122)	Customer OB Invoice		Inv 3098	Opening Balances Control Account (9998)		681.60	No
								Trade Debtors (1100)	681.60		No
5	21/04/2017	LH	30/04/2016	Ribbons & Curls (138)	Customer OB Invoice		Inv 3123	Opening Balances Control Account (9998)		391.20	No
								Trade Debtors (1100)	391.20		No
6	21/04/2017	LH	30/04/2016	Avada Cash & Carry (1134)	Supplier OB Invoice		Inv C/251	Trade Creditors (2100)		4,454.40	No
								Opening Balances Control Account (9998)	4,454.40		No
7	21/04/2017	LH	30/04/2016	Straightside Supplies (1138)	Supplier OB Invoice		Inv 9140	Trade Creditors (2100)		1,839.60	No
								Opening Balances Control Account (9998)	1,839.60		No
8	21/04/2017	LH	30/04/2016	Hair Supplies (1165)	Supplier OB Invoice		Inv 0028	Trade Creditors (2100)		818.40	No
								Opening Balances Control Account (9998)	818.40		No
9	21/04/2017	LH	30/04/2016	Wig Specialists (1185)	Supplier OB Invoice		Inv S653	Trade Creditors (2100)		102.00	No
								Opening Balances Control Account (9998)	102.00		No
10	21/04/2017	LH	30/04/2016		Bank Opening Balance			Opening Balances Control Account (9998)		54,210.81	No
								Current (1200)	54,210.81		Yes
11	21/04/2017	LH	30/04/2016		Bank Opening Balance			Opening Balances Control Account (9998)		200.00	No
								Petty Cash (1210)	200.00		No

From: 30/04/2016
To: 31/05/2016

Crazy Hair
Audit Trail Breakdown

25 Apr 2017
09:55

Trx No	Entry Date	User	Trx Date	Name	Type	Invoice Number	Ref	Ledger Account	Debit	Credit	Bank Reconciled
12	21/04/2017	LH	30/04/2016		Journal Opening Balance		OB 1/5/16	Motor Vehicles - Cost (0050)	24,000.00		No
								Opening Balances Control Account (9998)		24,000.00	No
								Fixtures and fittings - Cost (0040)	31,000.00		No
								Opening Balances Control Account (9998)		31,000.00	No
								VAT on Sales (2200)		5,550.00	No
								Opening Balances Control Account (9998)	5,550.00		No
								VAT on Purchases (2201)	1,507.94		No
								Opening Balances Control Account (9998)		1,507.94	No
								Capital introduced (3200)		165,000.00	No
								Opening Balances Control Account (9998)	165,000.00		No
								Drawings - equity (3260)	5,000.00		No
								Opening Balances Control Account (9998)		5,000.00	No
								Sales - Brushes (4000)		345.00	No
								Opening Balances Control Account (9998)	345.00		No
								Sales - Combs (4001)		187.00	No
								Opening Balances Control Account (9998)	187.00		No
								Sales - Colours (4002)		3,801.45	No
								Opening Balances Control Account (9998)	3,801.45		No
								Sales - Hairdryers (4003)		758.00	No
								Opening Balances Control Account (9998)	758.00		No
								Sales - Wigs (4004)		5,600.00	No
								Opening Balances Control Account (9998)	5,600.00		No
								Cash Sales (4005)		617.50	No
								Opening Balances Control Account (9998)	617.50		No
								Purchases - Brushes (5000)	873.00		No
								Opening Balances Control Account (9998)		873.00	No

From: 30/04/2016
To: 31/05/2016

Crazy Hair
Audit Trail Breakdown

25 Apr 2017
09:55

							Purchases - Combs (5001)	50.00		No
							Opening Balances Control Account (9998)		50.00	No
							Purchases - Colour (5002)	4,200.00		No
							Opening Balances Control Account (9998)		4,200.00	No
							Purchases - Hairdryers (5003)	6,310.00		No
							Opening Balances Control Account (9998)		6,310.00	No
							Purchases - Wigs (5004)	52,814.00		No
							Opening Balances Control Account (9998)		52,814.00	No
13	21/04/2017	LH	12/05/2016	Ribbons & Curls (138)	Sales QE Invoice	Inv 3353	Sales - Colours (4002)		141.00	No
							VAT on Sales (2200)		28.20	No
							Trade Debtors (1100)	169.20		No
14	21/04/2017	LH	12/05/2016	Alfred Images (104)	Sales QE Invoice	Inv 3354	Sales - Brushes (4000)		581.00	No
							VAT on Sales (2200)		116.20	No
							Trade Debtors (1100)	697.20		No
15	21/04/2017	LH	13/05/2016	Figgaro (110)	Sales QE Invoice	Inv 3355	Sales - Hairdryers (4003)		660.00	No
							VAT on Sales (2200)		132.00	No
							Trade Debtors (1100)	792.00		No
16	21/04/2017	LH	15/05/2016	Blades (118)	Sales QE Invoice	Inv 3356	Sales - Wigs (4004)		1,685.76	No
							VAT on Sales (2200)		337.15	No
							Trade Debtors (1100)	2,022.91		No
17	21/04/2017	LH	15/05/2016	Blades (118)	Sales QE Invoice	Inv 3356	Sales - Hairdryers (4003)		203.40	No
							VAT on Sales (2200)		40.68	No
							Trade Debtors (1100)	244.08		No
18	21/04/2017	LH	18/05/2016	Hair Studio (122)	Sales QE Invoice	Inv 3357	Sales - Brushes (4000)		316.80	No
							VAT on Sales (2200)		63.36	No
							Trade Debtors (1100)	380.16		No
19	21/04/2017	LH	18/05/2016	Hair Studio (122)	Sales QE Invoice	Inv 3357	Sales - Wigs (4004)		881.92	No
							VAT on Sales (2200)		176.38	No
							Trade Debtors (1100)	1,058.30		No
20	21/04/2017	LH	18/05/2016	Hair Studio (122)	Sales QE Invoice	Inv 3357	Sales - Colours (4002)		230.40	No
							VAT on Sales (2200)		46.08	No
							Trade Debtors (1100)	276.48		No
21	21/04/2017	LH	25/05/2016	Alfred Images (104)	Sales QE Credit	CN23	Trade Debtors (1100)		67.20	No
							Sales - Brushes (4000)	56.00		No
							VAT on Sales (2200)	11.20		No
22	21/04/2017	LH	11/05/2016	Straightside Supplies (1136)	Purchase QE Invoice	Inv 3362	Trade Creditors (2100)		229.92	No
							Purchases - Brushes (5000)	191.60		No
							VAT on Purchases (2201)	38.32		No
24	21/04/2017	LH	13/05/2016	Hair Supplies (1165)	Purchase QE Invoice	Inv 0814	Trade Creditors (2100)		178.56	No
							Purchases - Hairdryers (5003)	178.56		No
25	21/04/2017	LH	14/05/2016	Wig Specialists (1185)	Purchase QE Invoice	Inv S1196	Trade Creditors (2100)		4,072.32	No
							Purchases - Wigs (5004)	3,393.60		No
							VAT on Purchases (2201)	678.72		No
26	21/04/2017	LH	18/05/2016	Wig Specialists (1185)	Purchase QE Credit	C3223	Purchases - Wigs (5004)		102.70	No
							VAT on Purchases (2201)		20.54	No
							Trade Creditors (2100)	123.24		No
27	24/04/2017	LH	20/05/2016	Alfred Images (104)	Customer Receipt	Cheque no 183001	Trade Debtors (1100)		1,809.60	No

KAPLAN PUBLISHING

Crazy Hair
Audit Trail Breakdown

							Current (1200)	1,809.60		Yes
28	24/04/2017	LH	21/05/2016	Blades (118)	Customer Receipt	Chq no 654255	Trade Debtors (1100)		2,144.40	No
							Current (1200)	2,144.40		Yes
29	24/04/2017	LH	21/05/2016	Figgaro (110)	Customer Receipt	BACS	Trade Debtors (1100)		3,880.80	No
							Current (1200)	3,880.80		Yes
30	24/04/2017	LH	21/05/2016	Hair Studio (122)	Customer Receipt	Chq no 452221	Trade Debtors (1100)		681.60	No
							Current (1200)	681.60		Yes
31	24/04/2017	LH	31/05/2016	Wigs Specialist (1185)	Supplier Payment	Chq no 163455	Trade Creditors (2100)	102.00		No
							Current (1200)		102.00	No
32	24/04/2017	LH	31/05/2016	Avada Cash & Carry (1134)	Supplier Payment	Chq No 163456	Trade Creditors (2100)	4,454.40		No
							Current (1200)		4,454.40	No
33	24/04/2017	LH	31/05/2016	Hair Supplies (1165)	Supplier Payment	Chq no 163457	Trade Creditors (2100)	818.40		No
							Current (1200)		818.40	No
34	24/04/2017	LH	19/05/2016		Other Payment	CSH 86	Petty Cash (1210)		40.32	No
							Travel and Entertainment (7400)	33.60		No
							VAT on Purchases (2201)	6.72		No
35	24/04/2017	LH	20/05/2016		Other Payment	CSH 87	Petty Cash (1210)		4.51	No
							Office costs (7500)	4.51		No
36	24/04/2017	LH	20/05/2016		Other Receipt	1001	Sales - Brushes (4000)		17.50	No
							VAT on Sales (2200)		3.50	No
							Current (1200)	21.00		Yes
37	24/04/2017	LH	11/05/2016	Avada Cash & Carry (1134)	Purchase QE Invoice	Inv C/910	Trade Creditors (2100)		1,144.60	No
							Purchases - Colour (5002)	954.00		No
							VAT on Purchases (2201)	190.80		No
38	24/04/2017	LH	24/05/2016		Journal	JH12	Drawings - equity (3260)	440.00		No
							Current (1200)		440.00	Yes

From: 30/04/2016
To: 31/05/2016

Crazy Hair
Audit Trail Breakdown

25 Apr 2017
09:55

39	24/04/2017	LH	31/05/2016		Bank Transfer	TRF01	Current (1200)		30.52	Yes
							Petty Cash (1210)	30.52		No
40	25/04/2017	LH	31/05/2016		Bank Payment	Bank Charge	Current (1200)		27.11	Yes
							Bank charges and interest (7900)	27.11		No
41	25/04/2017	LH	24/05/2016		Other Payment	Coopers Union	Current (1200)		168.00	Yes
							Premises Insurance (7610)	168.00		No
42	25/04/2017	LH	31/05/2016		Other Payment	Electricity	Current (1200)		66.94	Yes
							Electricity (7200)	66.94		No

TASK 17

Aged Creditors (summary)

	Crazy Hair Aged Creditors Report					
To: 31/05/2016					25 Apr 2017 09:57	
Supplier	Credit limit	O/S Amt	< 30 days	< 60 days	< 90 days	Older
Avada Cash & Carry (1134)	£5,500.00	£1,144.80	£1,144.80	£0.00	£0.00	£0.00
Hair Supplies (1165)	£4,000.00	£178.56	£178.56	£0.00	£0.00	£0.00
Straightside Supplies (1138)	£12,000.00	£2,069.52	£229.92	£1,839.60	£0.00	£0.00
Wigs Specialist (1185)	£5,000.00	£3,949.08	£3,949.08	£0.00	£0.00	£0.00
	TOTAL	£7,341.96	£5,502.36	£1,839.60	£0.00	£0.00

TASK 17

Aged Debtors (summary)

	Crazy Hair Aged Debtors Report					
To: 31/05/2016					25 Apr 2017 09:58	
Customer	Credit limit	O/S Amt	< 30 days	< 60 days	< 90 days	Older
Alfred Images (104)	£8,000.00	£630.00	£630.00	£0.00	£0.00	£0.00
Blades (118)	£6,100.00	£2,266.99	£2,266.99	£0.00	£0.00	£0.00
Figgaro (110)	£6,500.00	£792.00	£792.00	£0.00	£0.00	£0.00
Hair Studio (122)	£5,000.00	£1,714.94	£1,714.94	£0.00	£0.00	£0.00
Ribbons & Curls (138)	£5,000.00	£560.40	£169.20	£391.20	£0.00	£0.00
	TOTAL	£5,964.33	£5,573.13	£391.20	£0.00	£0.00

 KAPLAN PUBLISHING

TASK 17

Nominal Ledger Activity Report for Bank Current Account and Petty Cash Account

From: 30/04/2016
To: 31/05/2016

Crazy Hair
Detailed Nominal Activity: Current (1200)

25 Apr 2017
10:00

Transaction Type: All

Trx No	Date	Invoice Number	Name	Type	Reference	Description	Debit	Credit	Running Total
						Opening Balance		0.00	
10	30/04/2016			Bank Opening Balance			54,210.81		54,210.81 Dr
27	20/05/2016		Alfred Images (104)	Customer Receipt	Cheque no 183001		1,809.60		56,020.41 Dr
36	20/05/2016			Other Receipt	1001		21.00		56,041.41 Dr
28	21/05/2016		Blades (118)	Customer Receipt	Chq no 654255		2,144.40		58,185.81 Dr
29	21/05/2016		Figgaro (110)	Customer Receipt	BACS		3,880.80		62,066.61 Dr
30	21/05/2016		Hair Studio (122)	Customer Receipt	Chq no 452221		681.60		62,748.21 Dr
38	24/05/2016			Journal	JH12			440.00	62,308.21 Dr
41	24/05/2016			Other Payment	Coopers Union			168.00	62,140.21 Dr
31	31/05/2016		Wigs Specialist (1185)	Supplier Payment	Chq no 163455			102.00	62,038.21 Dr
32	31/05/2016		Avada Cash & Carry (1134)	Supplier Payment	Chq No 163456			4,454.40	57,583.81 Dr
33	31/05/2016		Hair Supplies (1165)	Supplier Payment	Chq no 163457			818.40	56,765.41 Dr
39	31/05/2016			Bank Transfer	TRF01			30.52	56,734.89 Dr
40	31/05/2016			Bank Payment	Bank Charge			27.11	56,707.78 Dr
42	31/05/2016			Other Payment	Electricity			66.94	56,640.84 Dr
						Closing Balance	56,640.84		
						Period Variance	56,640.84		

From: 30/04/2016
To: 31/05/2016

Crazy Hair
Detailed Nominal Activity: Petty Cash (1210)

25 Apr 2017
10:04

Transaction Type: All

Trx No	Date	Invoice Number	Name	Type	Reference	Description	Debit	Credit	Running Total
						Opening Balance		0.00	
11	30/04/2016			Bank Opening Balance			200.00		200.00 Dr
34	19/05/2016			Other Payment	CSH 86			40.32	159.68 Dr
35	20/05/2016			Other Payment	CSH 87			4.51	155.17 Dr
39	31/05/2016			Bank Transfer	TRF01		30.52		185.69 Dr
						Closing Balance	185.69		
						Period Variance	185.69		

PRACTICE PAPER 3

SHOES 4U ANSWERS

TASK 3.3

Customer Address List

| | Shoes 4U | | | | 25 Apr 2017 |
| | Customer Address List | | | | 11:59 |

Address Types: All

Customer Name	Address	Contact name	Phone	Mobile	Email	Fax
Beckers Gate Ltd (SL186)	Butchergate Carlisle Cumbria C41 1SG	Main Contact				
Eaton Bowls Club (SL213)	Seaton Street St Neots Cambs PE19 8EF	Main Contact				
Jones Footwear (SL302)	Scotby Village Carlisle Cumbria C44 8BP	Main Contact				
Dickens Ladies Footwear (SL307)	17 Royal Square Bleachfield North Yorkshire YO87 9AD	Main Contact				

TASK 3.3

Supplier Address List

| | Shoes 4U | | | | 25 Apr 2017 |
| | Supplier Address List | | | | 12:01 |

Address Types: All

Supplier Name	Address	Contact name	Phone	Mobile	Email	Fax
Bootsy & Smudge Ltd (PL112)	Factory Road Stilton Cambs PE7 3RP	Main Contact				
Briggsthorpe Boots (PL168)	Long Buckby Wharf Long Buckby Northampton NN4 9UW	Main Contact				
Gallows Fashion (PL172)	18 The Crescent Pickford Cambs PE7 8QV	Main Contact				
Dickens Ladies Footwear (PL173)	17 Royal Square Bleachfield North Yorkshire YO87 9AD	Main Contact				

TASK 3.3

Trial Balance

From: 31/05/2016
To: 30/06/2016

Shoes 4U
Trial Balance Report

25 Apr 2017
12:03

This period only

Nominal Code	Name	Selected Period	
		Debit	Credit
0030	Freehold Property	72,000.00	
0040	Fixtures and fittings - Cost	9,000.00	
0050	Motor Vehicles - Cost	7,500.00	
1100	Trade Debtors	10,386.27	
1200	Current	14,363.00	
1210	Cash	200.00	
1220	Deposit	5,000.00	
2100	Trade Creditors		47,048.26
2200	VAT on Sales		3,402.35
2201	VAT on Purchases	1,130.00	
3200	Capital introduced		30,000.00
3260	Drawings - equity	600.00	
4000	Sales - Men's Footwear		79,320.00
4001	Sales - Ladies Footwear		43,210.00
4002	Cash Sales		6,798.00
5000	Purchases - Men's Footwear	55,432.00	
5001	Purchases - Ladies Footwear	23,410.00	
6200	Advertising	7,231.00	
7100	Rent	1,263.00	
7200	Electricity	567.34	
7500	Telephone	866.00	
7501	Office Stationery	830.00	
	TOTAL	£209,778.61	£209,778.61

TASK 7

Remittance Advices

Remittance Advice

Date Paid: 18/06/2016

Reference: PL172

Gallows Fashion
18 The Crescent
Pickford
Cambs
PE7 8QV

Shoes 4U
85 Barrington Close
Carlisle
Cumbria
C41 3ED
United Kingdom

Telephone: 01234 567891

VAT Number: GB 123456789

Reference: Chq no 109887

Our Ref	Your Ref	Date	Total Amount	Amount Paid
Inv G-01239		31/05/2016	400.00	400.00
			Total Paid:	**£ 400.00 GBP**

Remittance Advice

Date Paid: 18/06/2016

Reference: PL168

Briggsthorpe Boots
Long Buckby Wharf
Long Buckby
Northampton
NN4 9UW

Shoes 4U
85 Barrington Close
Carlisle
Cumbria
C41 3ED
United Kingdom

Telephone: 01234 567891

VAT Number: GB 123456789

Reference: Chq no 109888

Our Ref	Your Ref	Date	Total Amount	Amount Paid
Inv 0001087		31/05/2016	43,200.00	23,300.00
			Total Paid:	**£ 23,300.00 GBP**

TASK 10

Trial Balance

From: 31/05/2016
To: 30/06/2016

Shoes 4U
Trial Balance Report

25 Apr 2017
12:46

This period only

Nominal Code	Name	Debit	Credit
0030	Freehold Property	72,000.00	
0040	Fixtures and fittings - Cost	9,000.00	
0050	Motor Vehicles - Cost	7,500.00	
1100	Trade Debtors	6,874.56	
1200	Current	319.80	
1210	Cash	200.00	
1220	Deposit	5,000.00	
2100	Trade Creditors		29,948.26
2200	VAT on Sales		4,430.43
2201	VAT on Purchases	2,232.25	
3200	Capital introduced		30,000.00
3260	Drawings - equity	600.00	
4000	Sales - Men's Footwear		81,669.66
4001	Sales - Ladies Footwear		46,000.75
4002	Cash Sales		6,798.00
5000	Purchases - Men's Footwear	60,432.00	
5001	Purchases - Ladies Footwear	23,910.00	
6200	Advertising	7,231.00	
7100	Rent	1,263.00	
7200	Electricity	567.34	
7500	Telephone	866.00	
7501	Office Stationery	841.25	
7502	Refreshments	9.90	
	TOTAL	£198,847.10	£198,847.10

TASK 10

Sales Day Book

From: 31/05/2016
To: 30/06/2016

Shoes 4U
Sales Day Book Report

25 Apr 2017
12:48

Type: Sales QE Invoice

Trx No	Type	Date	Name	Invoice Number	Ref	Details	Net	VAT	Total
13	Sales QE Invoice	04/06/2016	Beckers Gate Ltd		Inv 1622		450.00	90.00	540.00
14	Sales QE Invoice	06/06/2016	Eaton Bowls Club		Inv 1623		1,385.00	277.00	1,662.00
15	Sales QE Invoice	14/06/2016	Dickens Ladies Footwear		Inv 1624		450.00	90.00	540.00
16	Sales QE Invoice	14/06/2016	Dickens Ladies Footwear		Inv 1624		1,850.00	370.00	2,220.00
17	Sales QE Invoice	17/06/2016	Jones Footwear		Inv 1625		1,175.75	235.15	1,410.90
						TOTAL	£5,310.75	£1,062.15	£6,372.90

TASK 10

Customer Activity Report

From: 31/05/2016
To: 30/06/2016

Shoes 4U
Customer Activity Report

25 Apr 2017
12:49

Beckers Gate Ltd (SL186)

Date	Number	Reference	Type	Net	VAT	Total	Discount	Outstanding
31/05/2016		Inv 1613	Customer OB Invoice	4,811.88	0.00	4,811.88		0.00
04/06/2016		Inv 1622	Sales QE Invoice	450.00	90.00	540.00		540.00
11/06/2016		Chq no 199846	Customer Receipt			-4,811.88	0.00	0.00
						540.00		**540.00**

Eaton Bowls Club (SL213)

Date	Number	Reference	Type	Net	VAT	Total	Discount	Outstanding
31/05/2016		Inv 1582	Customer OB Invoice	961.98	0.00	961.98		0.00
06/06/2016		Inv 1623	Sales QE Invoice	1,385.00	277.00	1,662.00		1,662.00
14/06/2016		Chq No 107654	Customer Receipt			-961.98	0.00	0.00
						1,662.00		**1,662.00**

Jones Footwear (SL302)

Date	Number	Reference	Type	Net	VAT	Total	Discount	Outstanding
31/05/2016		Inv 1596	Customer OB Invoice	3,828.75	0.00	3,828.75		0.00
14/06/2016		244536	Customer Receipt			-3,828.75	0.00	0.00
17/06/2016		Inv 1625	Sales QE Invoice	1,175.75	235.15	1,410.90		1,410.90
						1,410.90		**1,410.90**

Dickens Ladies Footwear (SL307)

Date	Number	Reference	Type	Net	VAT	Total	Discount	Outstanding
31/05/2016		Inv 1601	Customer OB Invoice	783.66	0.00	783.66		783.66
08/06/2016		Credit note no CR10	Sales QE Credit	-235.00	-47.00	-282.00		-282.00
14/06/2016		Inv 1624	Sales QE Invoice	450.00	90.00	540.00		540.00
14/06/2016		Inv 1624	Sales QE Invoice	1,850.00	370.00	2,220.00		2,220.00
						3,261.66		**3,261.66**

TASK 10

Supplier Activity Report

Shoes 4U
Supplier Activity Report

Bootsy & Smudge Ltd (PL112)

Date	Number	Reference	Type	Net	VAT	Total	Discount	Outstanding
31/05/2016		Inv B/468	Supplier OB Invoice	2,881.26	0.00	2,881.26		2,881.26
02/06/2016		Inv B/752	Purchase QE Invoice	300.00	60.00	360.00		360.00
13/06/2016		inv B/753	Purchase QE Invoice	200.00	40.00	240.00		240.00
						3,481.26		**3,481.26**

Briggsthorpe Boots (PL168)

Date	Number	Reference	Type	Net	VAT	Total	Discount	Outstanding
31/05/2016		Inv 0001087	Supplier OB Invoice	43,200.00	0.00	43,200.00		19,900.00
10/06/2016		Inv 12350	Purchase QE Invoice	2,500.00	500.00	3,000.00		3,000.00
18/06/2016		Chq no 109888	Supplier Payment			-23,300.00	0.00	0.00
						22,900.00		**22,900.00**

Gallows Fashion (PL172)

Date	Number	Reference	Type	Net	VAT	Total	Discount	Outstanding
31/05/2016		Inv G-01239	Supplier OB Invoice	400.00	0.00	400.00		0.00
12/06/2016		Inv G-2285	Purchase QE Invoice	2,500.00	500.00	3,000.00		3,000.00
18/06/2016		Chq no 109887	Supplier Payment			-400.00	0.00	0.00
						3,000.00		**3,000.00**

Dickens Ladies Footwear (PL173)

Date	Number	Reference	Type	Net	VAT	Total	Discount	Outstanding
31/05/2016		Inv 06345	Supplier OB Invoice	567.00	0.00	567.00		567.00
						567.00		**567.00**

TASK 10

Aged Creditors Report (detailed)

Shoes 4U
Aged Creditors Breakdown

Date	Reference	Total	Due Date	O/S Amt	< 30 days	< 60 days	< 90 days	Older
Bootsy & Smudge Ltd (PL112), Credit limit: £4,000.00								
, Terms: 30 days - OVERDUE								
31/05/2016	Inv B/468	2,881.26	30/06/2016	2,881.26		2,881.26		
02/06/2016	Inv B/752	360.00	02/07/2016	360.00	360.00			
13/06/2016	inv B/753	240.00	13/07/2016	240.00	240.00			
				£3,481.26	£600.00	£2,881.26	£0.00	£0.00
Briggsthorpe Boots (PL168), Credit limit: £50,000.00								
, Terms: 30 days - OVERDUE								
31/05/2016	Inv 0001087	43,200.00	30/06/2016	19,900.00		19,900.00		
10/06/2016	Inv 12350	3,000.00	10/07/2016	3,000.00	3,000.00			
				£22,900.00	£3,000.00	£19,900.00	£0.00	£0.00
Dickens Ladies Footwear (PL173), Credit limit: £2,000.00								
, Terms: 30 days - OVERDUE								
31/05/2016	Inv 06345	567.00	30/06/2016	567.00		567.00		
				£567.00	£0.00	£567.00	£0.00	£0.00
Gallows Fashion (PL172), Credit limit: £2,000.00								
, Terms: 30 days - OVERDUE								
12/06/2016	Inv G-2285	3,000.00	12/07/2016	3,000.00	3,000.00			
				£3,000.00	£3,000.00	£0.00	£0.00	£0.00
			TOTAL	**£29,948.26**	**£6,600.00**	**£23,348.26**	**£0.00**	**£0.00**

TASK 10

Aged Debtors Report (detailed)

Date	Reference	Total	Due Date	O/S Amt	< 30 days	< 60 days	< 90 days	Older
Beckers Gate Ltd (SL186), Credit limit: £5,000.00								
, Terms: 30 days - OVERDUE								
04/06/2016	QE-Inv 1622	540.00	04/07/2016	540.00	540.00			
				£540.00	£540.00	£0.00	£0.00	£0.00
Dickens Ladies Footwear (SL307), Credit limit: £11,000.00								
, Terms: 30 days - OVERDUE								
31/05/2016	OB-Inv 1601	783.66	30/06/2016	783.66		783.66		
08/06/2016	QE-Credit note no CR10	-282.00		-282.00	-282.00			
14/06/2016	QE-Inv 1624	540.00	14/07/2016	540.00	540.00			
14/06/2016	QE-Inv 1624	2,220.00	14/07/2016	2,220.00	2,220.00			
				£3,261.66	£2,478.00	£783.66	£0.00	£0.00
Eaton Bowls Club (SL213), Credit limit: £3,000.00								
, Terms: 30 days - OVERDUE								
06/06/2016	QE-Inv 1623	1,662.00	06/07/2016	1,662.00	1,662.00			
				£1,662.00	£1,662.00	£0.00	£0.00	£0.00
Jones Footwear (SL302), Credit limit: £6,000.00								
, Terms: 30 days - OVERDUE								
17/06/2016	QE-Inv 1625	1,410.90	17/07/2016	1,410.90	1,410.90			
				£1,410.90	£1,410.90	£0.00	£0.00	£0.00
			TOTAL	£6,874.56	£6,090.90	£783.66	£0.00	£0.00

TASK 10

Nominal Ledger Activity Report for Bank Current Account and Petty Cash Account

From: 31/05/2016
To: 30/06/2016

Shoes 4U
Detailed Nominal Activity: Current (1200)

25 Apr 2017
13:33

Transaction Type: All

Trx No	Date	Invoice Number	Name	Type	Reference	Description	Debit	Credit	Running Total
						Opening Balance		0.00	
9	31/05/2016			Bank Opening Balance			19,363.00		19,363.00 Dr
12	01/06/2016			Bank Transfer	TRF01			5,000.00	14,363.00 Dr
30	10/06/2016			Bank Transfer	TRF02			23.40	14,339.60 Dr
23	11/06/2016		Beckers Gate Ltd (SL186)	Customer Receipt	Chq no 199846		4,811.88		19,151.48 Dr
24	14/06/2016		Eaton Bowls Club (SL213)	Customer Receipt	Chq No 107654		961.98		20,113.46 Dr
25	14/06/2016		Jones Footwear (SL302)	Customer Receipt	244536		3,828.75		23,942.21 Dr
26	18/06/2016		Gallows Fashion (PL172)	Supplier Payment	Chq no 109887			400.00	23,542.21 Dr
27	18/06/2016		Briggsthorpe Boots (PL168)	Supplier Payment	Chq no 109888			23,300.00	242.21 Dr
31	23/06/2016			Other Receipt	F027		77.59		319.80 Dr
						Closing Balance	319.80		
						Period Variance	319.80		

From: 31/05/2016
To: 30/06/2016

Shoes 4U
Detailed Nominal Activity: Cash (1210)

25 Apr 2017
13:35

Transaction Type: All

Trx No	Date	Invoice Number	Name	Type	Reference	Description	Debit	Credit	Running Total
						Opening Balance		0.00	
10	31/05/2016			Bank Opening Balance			200.00		200.00 Dr
28	05/06/2016			Other Payment	Voucher no 010			9.90	190.10 Dr
29	10/06/2016			Other Payment	Voucher no 011			13.50	176.60 Dr
30	10/06/2016			Bank Transfer	TRF02		23.40		200.00 Dr
						Closing Balance	200.00		
						Period Variance	200.00		

TASK 11.1

Recurring payment

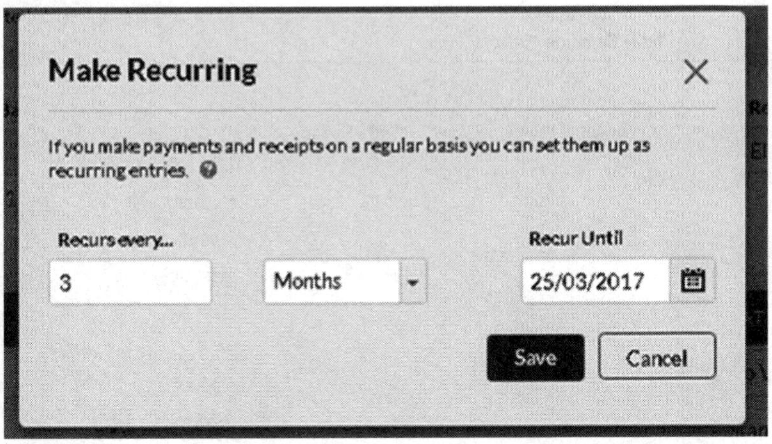

Task 11.2

Recurring receipt

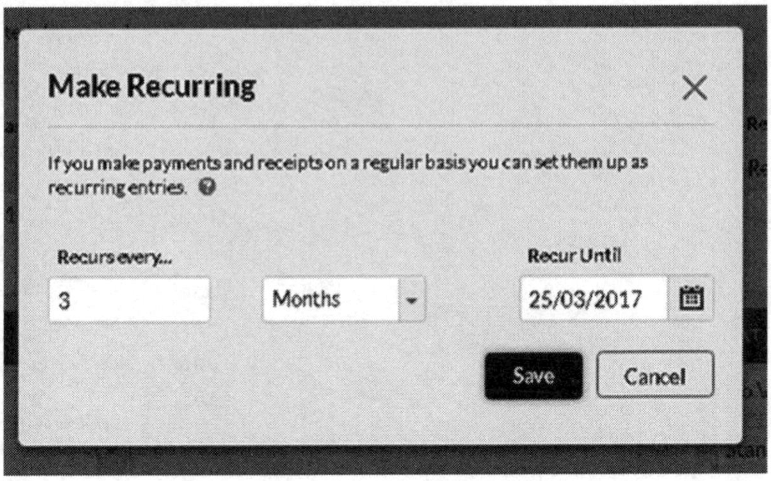

TASK 15

Trial Balance

From: 31/05/2016
To: 30/06/2016

Shoes 4U
Trial Balance Report

25 Apr 2017
14:16

This period only

Nominal Code	Name	Selected Period	
		Debit	Credit
0030	Freehold Property	72,000.00	
0040	Fixtures and fittings - Cost	9,000.00	
0050	Motor Vehicles - Cost	7,500.00	
1100	Trade Debtors	6,874.56	
1200	Current		1,569.20
1210	Cash	200.00	
1220	Deposit	5,000.00	
2100	Trade Creditors		29,948.26
2200	VAT on Sales		4,439.43
2201	VAT on Purchases	2,232.25	
3200	Capital introduced		30,000.00
3260	Drawings - equity	3,800.00	
4000	Sales - Men's Footwear		81,669.66
4001	Sales - Ladies Footwear		46,045.75
4002	Cash Sales		6,798.00
4900	Other income		1,500.00
5000	Purchases - Men's Footwear	60,432.00	
5001	Purchases - Ladies Footwear	23,910.00	
6200	Advertising	7,231.00	
7100	Rent	1,263.00	
7200	Electricity	760.34	
7500	Telephone	866.00	
7501	Office Stationery	841.25	
7502	Refreshments	9.90	
7900	Bank charges and interest	50.00	
	TOTAL	£201,970.30	£201,970.30

TASK 15

Audit Trail

From: 31/05/2016
To: 30/06/2016

Shoes 4U
Audit Trail Breakdown

25 Apr 2017
14:18

Type: All, Status: All

Trx No	Entry Date	User	Trx Date	Name	Type	Invoice Number	Ref	Ledger Account	Debit	Credit	Bank Reconciled
1	25/04/2017	LH	31/05/2016	Beckers Gate Ltd (SL186)	Customer OB Invoice		Inv 1613	Opening Balances Control Account (9996)		4,811.88	No
								Trade Debtors (1100)	4,811.88		No
2	25/04/2017	LH	31/05/2016	Eaton Bowls Club (SL213)	Customer OB Invoice		Inv 1582	Opening Balances Control Account (9996)		961.98	No
								Trade Debtors (1100)	961.98		No
3	25/04/2017	LH	31/05/2016	Jones Footwear (SL302)	Customer OB Invoice		Inv 1596	Opening Balances Control Account (9996)		3,828.75	No
								Trade Debtors (1100)	3,828.75		No
4	25/04/2017	LH	31/05/2016	Dickens Ladies Footwear (SL307)	Customer OB Invoice		Inv 1601	Opening Balances Control Account (9996)		783.66	No
								Trade Debtors (1100)	783.66		No
5	25/04/2017	LH	31/05/2016	Bootsy & Smudge Ltd (PL112)	Supplier OB Invoice		Inv B/468	Trade Creditors (2100)		2,881.26	No
								Opening Balances Control Account (9996)	2,881.26		No
6	25/04/2017	LH	31/05/2016	Briggsthorpe Boots (PL168)	Supplier OB Invoice		Inv 0001087	Trade Creditors (2100)		43,200.00	No
								Opening Balances Control Account (9996)	43,200.00		No
7	25/04/2017	LH	31/05/2016	Gallows Fashion (PL172)	Supplier OB Invoice		Inv G-01239	Trade Creditors (2100)		400.00	No
								Opening Balances Control Account (9996)	400.00		No
8	25/04/2017	LH	31/05/2016	Dickens Ladies Footwear (PL173)	Supplier OB Invoice		Inv 06345	Trade Creditors (2100)		567.00	No
								Opening Balances Control Account (9996)	567.00		No
9	25/04/2017	LH	31/05/2016		Bank Opening Balance			Opening Balances Control Account (9996)		19,363.00	No
								Current (1200)	19,363.00		Yes
10	25/04/2017	LH	31/05/2016		Bank Opening Balance			Opening Balances Control Account (9996)		200.00	No
								Cash (1210)	200.00		No
11	25/04/2017	LH	31/05/2016		Journal Opening Balance		OB 1/6/16	Freehold Property (0030)	72,000.00		No
								Opening Balances Control Account (9996)		72,000.00	No

From: 31/05/2016
To: 30/06/2016

Shoes 4U
Audit Trail Breakdown

25 Apr 2017
14:18

	Ledger Account	Debit	Credit	Bank Reconciled
	Motor Vehicles - Cost (0050)	7,500.00		No
	Opening Balances Control Account (9996)		7,500.00	No
	Fixtures and fittings - Cost (0040)	9,000.00		No
	Opening Balances Control Account (9996)		9,000.00	No
	VAT on Sales (2200)		3,402.35	No
	Opening Balances Control Account (9996)	3,402.35		No
	VAT on Purchases (2201)	1,130.00		No
	Opening Balances Control Account (9996)		1,130.00	No
	Capital introduced (3200)		30,000.00	No
	Opening Balances Control Account (9996)	30,000.00		No
	Drawings - equity (3260)	600.00		No
	Opening Balances Control Account (9996)		600.00	No
	Sales - Men's Footwear (4000)		79,320.00	No
	Opening Balances Control Account (9996)	79,320.00		No
	Sales - Ladies Footwear (4001)		43,210.00	No
	Opening Balances Control Account (9996)	43,210.00		No
	Cash Sales (4002)		6,798.00	No
	Opening Balances Control Account (9996)	6,798.00		No
	Purchases - Men's Footwear (5000)	55,432.00		No
	Opening Balances Control Account (9996)		55,432.00	No
	Purchases - Ladies Footwear (5001)	23,410.00		No
	Opening Balances Control Account (9996)		23,410.00	No
	Advertising (6200)	7,231.00		No
	Opening Balances Control Account (9996)		7,231.00	No
	Telephone (7500)	866.00		No
	Opening Balances Control Account (9996)		866.00	No

From: 31/05/2016
To: 30/06/2016
                    Shoes 4U
              Audit Trail Breakdown
                                          25 Apr 2017
                                          14:18

							Rent (7100)	1,263.00		No
							Opening Balances Control Account (9998)		1,263.00	No
							Electricity (7200)	567.34		No
							Opening Balances Control Account (9998)		567.34	No
							Office Stationery (7501)	830.00		No
							Opening Balances Control Account (9998)		830.00	No
12	25/04/2017	LH	01/06/2016		Bank Transfer	TRF01	Current (1200)		5,000.00	Yes
							Deposit (1220)	5,000.00		No
13	25/04/2017	LH	04/06/2016	Beckers Gate Ltd (SL186)	Sales QE Invoice	Inv 1622	Sales - Men's Footwear (4000)		450.00	No
							VAT on Sales (2200)		90.00	No
							Trade Debtors (1100)	540.00		No
14	25/04/2017	LH	06/06/2016	Eaton Bowls Club (SL213)	Sales QE Invoice	Inv 1623	Sales - Men's Footwear (4000)		1,385.00	No
							VAT on Sales (2200)		277.00	No
							Trade Debtors (1100)	1,662.00		No
15	25/04/2017	LH	14/06/2016	Dickens Ladies Footwear (SL307)	Sales QE Invoice	Inv 1624	Sales - Men's Footwear (4000)		450.00	No
							VAT on Sales (2200)		90.00	No
							Trade Debtors (1100)	540.00		No
16	25/04/2017	LH	14/06/2016	Dickens Ladies Footwear (SL307)	Sales QE Invoice	Inv 1624	Sales - Ladies Footwear (4001)		1,850.00	No
							VAT on Sales (2200)		370.00	No
							Trade Debtors (1100)	2,220.00		No
17	25/04/2017	LH	17/06/2016	Jones Footwear (SL302)	Sales QE Invoice	Inv 1625	Sales - Ladies Footwear (4001)		1,175.75	No
							VAT on Sales (2200)		235.15	No
							Trade Debtors (1100)	1,410.90		No
18	25/04/2017	LH	08/06/2016	Dickens Ladies Footwear (SL307)	Sales QE Credit	Credit note no CR10	Trade Debtors (1100)		282.00	No
							Sales - Ladies Footwear (4001)	235.00		No
							VAT on Sales (2200)	47.00		No

From: 31/05/2016
To: 30/06/2016
                    Shoes 4U
              Audit Trail Breakdown
                                          25 Apr 2017
                                          14:18

19	25/04/2017	LH	02/06/2016	Bootsy & Smudge Ltd (PL112)	Purchase QE Invoice	Inv B/752	Trade Creditors (2100)		360.00	No
							Purchases - Ladies Footwear (5001)	300.00		No
							VAT on Purchases (2201)	60.00		No
20	25/04/2017	LH	10/06/2016	Briggsthorpe Boots (PL168)	Purchase QE Invoice	Inv 12350	Trade Creditors (2100)		3,000.00	No
							Purchases - Men's Footwear (5000)	2,500.00		No
							VAT on Purchases (2201)	500.00		No
21	25/04/2017	LH	12/06/2016	Gallows Fashion (PL172)	Purchase QE Invoice	Inv G-2285	Trade Creditors (2100)		3,000.00	No
							Purchases - Men's Footwear (5000)	2,500.00		No
							VAT on Purchases (2201)	500.00		No
22	25/04/2017	LH	13/06/2016	Bootsy & Smudge Ltd (PL112)	Purchase QE Invoice	inv B/753	Trade Creditors (2100)		240.00	No
							Purchases - Ladies Footwear (5001)	200.00		No
							VAT on Purchases (2201)	40.00		No
23	25/04/2017	LH	11/06/2016	Beckers Gate Ltd (SL186)	Customer Receipt	Chq no 199846	Trade Debtors (1100)		4,811.88	No
							Current (1200)	4,811.88		Yes
24	25/04/2017	LH	14/06/2016	Eaton Bowls Club (SL213)	Customer Receipt	Chq No 107654	Trade Debtors (1100)		961.98	No
							Current (1200)	961.98		Yes
25	25/04/2017	LH	14/06/2016	Jones Footwear (SL302)	Customer Receipt	244536	Trade Debtors (1100)		3,828.75	No
							Current (1200)	3,828.75		Yes
26	25/04/2017	LH	18/06/2016	Gallows Fashion (PL172)	Supplier Payment	Chq no 109887	Trade Creditors (2100)	400.00		No
							Current (1200)		400.00	No
27	25/04/2017	LH	18/06/2016	Briggsthorpe Boots (PL168)	Supplier Payment	Chq no 109888	Trade Creditors (2100)	23,300.00		No
							Current (1200)		23,300.00	Yes
28	25/04/2017	LH	05/06/2016		Other Payment	Voucher no 010	Cash (1210)		9.90	No
							Refreshments (7502)	9.90		No
29	25/04/2017	LH	10/06/2016		Other Payment	Voucher no 011	Cash (1210)		13.50	No
							Office Stationery (7501)	11.25		No

| From: 31/05/2016 To: 30/06/2016 | | | | Shoes 4U **Audit Trail Breakdown** | | | | 25 Apr 2017 14:18 |

							VAT on Purchases (2201)		2.25		No
30	25/04/2017	LH	10/06/2016		Bank Transfer	TRF02	Current (1200)			23.40	Yes
							Cash (1210)	23.40			No
31	25/04/2017	LH	23/06/2016		Other Receipt	F027	Sales - Men's Footwear (4000)			64.66	No
							VAT on Sales (2200)			12.93	No
							Current (1200)		77.59		Yes
42	25/04/2017	LH	25/06/2016		Journal	JNL 209	Drawings - equity (3260)	3,200.00			No
							Current (1200)			3,200.00	Yes
43	25/04/2017	LH	22/06/2016		Other Receipt	DC03	Sales - Ladies Footwear (4001)			45.00	No
							VAT on Sales (2200)			9.00	No
							Current (1200)		54.00		Yes

| From: 31/05/2016 To: 30/06/2016 | | | | Shoes 4U **Audit Trail Breakdown** | | | | 25 Apr 2017 14:18 |

44	25/04/2017	LH	25/06/2016		Bank Payment	Bank Charge	Current (1200)			50.00	Yes
							Bank charges and interest (7900)	50.00			No
47	25/04/2017	LH	25/06/2016		Other Receipt	Rent	Other income (4900)			1,500.00	No
							Current (1200)	1,500.00			Yes
48	25/04/2017	LH	25/06/2016		Other Payment	Electricity	Current (1200)			193.00	Yes
							Electricity (7200)	193.00			No

Task 15

Nominal Ledger Activity Report for Trade Creditors and Sales – Ladies Footwear

| From: 31/05/2016 To: 30/06/2016 | | | Shoes 4U **Detailed Nominal Activity: Trade Creditors (2100)** | | | | | 25 Apr 2017 14:23 |

Transaction Type: All

Trx No	Date	Invoice Number	Name	Type	Reference	Description	Debit	Credit	Running Total
						Opening Balance		0.00	
5	31/05/2016		Bootsy & Smudge Ltd (PL112)	Supplier OB Invoice	Inv B/468			2,881.26	2,881.26 Cr
6	31/05/2016		Briggsthorpe Boots (PL168)	Supplier OB Invoice	Inv 0001087			43,200.00	46,081.26 Cr
7	31/05/2016		Gallows Fashion (PL172)	Supplier OB Invoice	Inv G-01239			400.00	46,481.26 Cr
8	31/05/2016		Dickens Ladies Footwear (PL173)	Supplier OB Invoice	Inv 06345			567.00	47,048.26 Cr
19	02/06/2016		Bootsy & Smudge Ltd (PL112)	Purchase QE Invoice	Inv B/752			360.00	47,408.26 Cr
20	10/06/2016		Briggsthorpe Boots (PL168)	Purchase QE Invoice	Inv 12350			3,000.00	50,408.26 Cr
21	12/06/2016		Gallows Fashion (PL172)	Purchase QE Invoice	Inv G-2285			3,000.00	53,408.26 Cr
22	13/06/2016		Bootsy & Smudge Ltd (PL112)	Purchase QE Invoice	inv B/753			240.00	53,648.26 Cr
26	18/06/2016		Gallows Fashion (PL172)	Supplier Payment	Chq no 109887		400.00		53,248.26 Cr
27	18/06/2016		Briggsthorpe Boots (PL168)	Supplier Payment	Chq no 109888		23,300.00		29,948.26 Cr
						Closing Balance		29,948.26	
						Period Variance		29,948.26	

| From: 31/05/2016 To: 30/06/2016 | | | Shoes 4U **Detailed Nominal Activity: Sales - Ladies Footwear (4001)** | | | | | 25 Apr 2017 14:25 |

Transaction Type: All

Trx No	Date	Invoice Number	Name	Type	Reference	Description	Debit	Credit	Running Total
						Opening Balance		0.00	
11	31/05/2016			Journal Opening Balance	OB 1/6/16	(Opening Balance)		43,210.00	43,210.00 Cr
18	08/06/2016		Dickens Ladies Footwear (SL307)	Sales QE Credit	Credit note no CR10		235.00		42,975.00 Cr
16	14/06/2016		Dickens Ladies Footwear (SL307)	Sales QE Invoice	Inv 1624			1,850.00	44,825.00 Cr
17	17/06/2016		Jones Footwear (SL302)	Sales QE Invoice	Inv 1625			1,175.75	46,000.75 Cr
43	22/06/2016			Other Receipt	DC03	paid by debit card		45.00	46,045.75 Cr
						Closing Balance		46,045.75	
						Period Variance		46,045.75	

TASK 15

Aged Debtors Analysis

To: 30/06/2016		Shoes 4U **Aged Debtors Breakdown**					25 Apr 2017 14:27	
Date	Reference	Total	Due Date	O/S Amt	< 30 days	< 60 days	< 90 days	Older
Beckers Gate Ltd (SL186), Credit limit: £5,000.00 , Terms: 30 days - OVERDUE								
04/06/2016	QE-Inv 1622	540.00	04/07/2016	540.00	540.00			
				£540.00	£540.00	£0.00	£0.00	£0.00
Dickens Ladies Footwear (SL307), Credit limit: £11,000.00 , Terms: 30 days - OVERDUE								
31/05/2016	OB-Inv 1601	783.66	30/06/2016	783.66		783.66		
08/06/2016	QE-Credit note no CR10	-282.00		-282.00	-282.00			
14/06/2016	QE-Inv 1624	540.00	14/07/2016	540.00	540.00			
14/06/2016	QE-Inv 1624	2,220.00	14/07/2016	2,220.00	2,220.00			
				£3,261.66	£2,478.00	£783.66	£0.00	£0.00
Eaton Bowls Club (SL213), Credit limit: £3,000.00 , Terms: 30 days - OVERDUE								
06/06/2016	QE-Inv 1623	1,662.00	06/07/2016	1,662.00	1,662.00			
				£1,662.00	£1,662.00	£0.00	£0.00	£0.00
Jones Footwear (SL302), Credit limit: £6,000.00 , Terms: 30 days - OVERDUE								
17/06/2016	QE-Inv 1625	1,410.90	17/07/2016	1,410.90	1,410.90			
				£1,410.90	£1,410.90	£0.00	£0.00	£0.00
			TOTAL	£6,874.56	£6,090.90	£783.66	£0.00	£0.00

PRACTICE PAPER 4

SPORTS GEAR ANSWERS

TASK 3.2

Customer Address List

| | Sports Gear | 25 Apr 2017 |
| | Customer Address List | 15:30 |

Address Types: All

Customer Name	Address	Contact name	Phone	Mobile	Email	Fax
J Hollingham (SL01)	56 Glencoe Avenue Gants Hill Ilford Essex IG1 6FR	Main Contact				
Paul McCallum (SL02)	St Albans Road Seven Kings Essex IG7 8DS	Main Contact				
Kerry Jenkins (SL03)	34 Gloucester Road Gillingham Kent ME14 3TL	Main Contact				
Harry Bucket (SL04)	54 Dale Road Harrogate North Yorks YO2 3HN	Main Contact				
Evelyn Rose (SL05)	98 Crabtree Drive Bromley Kent DA3 6AY	Main Contact				

TASK 3.2

Supplier Address List

| | Sports Gear | 25 Apr 2017 |
| | Supplier Address List | 15:31 |

Address Types: All

Supplier Name	Address	Contact name	Phone	Mobile	Email	Fax
Radcliff and Sons (PL01)	Orient House Lower Clapham London E1 2RH	Main Contact				
Tennison Bros (PL02)	White Cottage London WC1 6YD	Main Contact				
Skipton & Co (PL03)	22 Chatsworth Lane Water Square London EC1V 6NU	Main Contact				
Evelyn Rose (PL04)	98 Crabtree Drive Bromley Kent DA3 6AY	Main Contact				

TASK 3.2

Trial Balance

From: 30/06/2016
To: 31/07/2016

Sports Gear
Trial Balance Report

25 Apr 2017
15:28

This period only

Nominal Code	Name	Selected Period	
		Debit	Credit
0030	Office equipment - Cost	8,430.00	
0040	Fixtures and fittings - Cost	18,000.00	
0050	Motor Vehicles - Cost	15,500.00	
1100	Trade Debtors	8,445.46	
1200	Current	3,325.40	
1210	Cash	300.00	
2100	Trade Creditors		8,914.14
2200	VAT on Sales		3,458.00
2201	VAT on Purchases	1,120.00	
3200	Capital introduced		52,000.00
3260	Drawings - equity	1,294.00	
4000	Sales - Tennis Racquets		13,266.78
4001	Sales - Exercise Bikes		22,310.00
4002	Sales - Golf Clubs		9,543.00
4003	Sales - Fishing Rods		5,644.00
5000	Purchases - Tennis Racquets	21,354.00	
5001	Purchases - Exercise Bikes	25,610.00	
5002	Purchases - Golf Clubs	5,475.00	
5003	Purchases - Fishing Rods	4,796.00	
7200	Electricity	496.06	
7500	Office Stationery	430.00	
7501	Postage	560.00	
	TOTAL	£115,135.92	£115,135.92

TASK 8

Remittance Advices

Remittance Advice

Date Paid: 14/07/2016

Reference: PL01

Radcliff and Sons
Orient House
Lower Clapham
London
E1 2RH

Sports Gear
34 Hockey Avenue
Tennison
London
EC1V 1NY
United Kingdom

Telephone: 01234 567891

VAT Number: GB 123456789

Reference: Chq no 170012

Our Ref	Your Ref	Date	Total Amount	Amount Paid
Inv 1874		30/06/2016	5,362.14	5,362.14
			Total Paid:	£ 5,362.14 GBP

Remittance Advice

Date Paid: 17/07/2016

Reference: PL02

Tennison Bros
White Cottage
London
WC1 6YD

Sports Gear
34 Hockey Avenue
Tennison
London
EC1V 1NY
United Kingdom

Telephone: 01234 567891

VAT Number: GB 123456789

Reference: Chq no 170013

Our Ref	Your Ref	Date	Total Amount	Amount Paid
Inv B-321		30/06/2016	2,801.00	2,801.00
			Total Paid:	£ 2,801.00 GBP

TASK 11

Trial Balance

From: 30/06/2016
To: 31/07/2016

Sports Gear
Trial Balance Report

25 Apr 2017
16:09

This period only

Nominal Code	Name	Selected Period	
		Debit	Credit
0030	Office equipment - Cost	8,430.00	
0040	Fixtures and fittings - Cost	18,000.00	
0050	Motor Vehicles - Cost	15,500.00	
1100	Trade Debtors	6,108.50	
1200	Current	6,811.61	
1210	Cash		132.16
2100	Trade Creditors		3,629.46
2200	VAT on Sales		5,010.07
2201	VAT on Purchases	1,662.62	
3200	Capital introduced		52,000.00
3260	Drawings - equity	1,294.00	
4000	Sales – Tennis Racquets		16,276.83
4001	Sales - Exercise Bikes		25,222.47
4002	Sales - Golf Clubs		11,056.80
4003	Sales - Fishing Rods		5,968.00
5000	Purchases - Tennis Racquets	21,904.00	
5001	Purchases - Exercise Bikes	25,930.00	
5002	Purchases - Golf Clubs	6,303.55	
5003	Purchases - Fishing Rods	5,467.00	
7200	Electricity	496.06	
7500	Office Stationery	449.90	
7501	Postage	938.55	
	TOTAL	**£119,295.79**	**£119,295.79**

TASK 11

Sales Day Book

	From: 30/06/2016 To: 31/07/2016			Sports Gear **Sales Day Book Report**						25 Apr 2017 16:10

Type: Sales QE Invoice

Trx No	Type	Date	Name	Invoice Number	Ref	Details	Net	VAT	Total
13	Sales QE Invoice	04/07/2016	J Hollingham		Inv 1052		682.00	176.40	1,058.40
14	Sales QE Invoice	04/07/2016	J Hollingham		Inv 1052		1,023.60	204.72	1,228.32
15	Sales QE Invoice	04/07/2016	J Hollingham		Inv 1052		324.00	64.80	388.80
16	Sales QE Invoice	06/07/2016	Kerry Jenkins		Inv 1053		132.30	26.46	158.76
17	Sales QE Invoice	08/07/2016	Harry Bucket		Inv 1054		1,513.80	302.76	1,816.56
						TOTAL	£3,875.70	£775.14	£4,650.84

TASK 11

Purchase Day Book

	From: 30/06/2016 To: 31/07/2016			Sports Gear **Purchase Day Book Report**						25 Apr 2017 16:11

Type: Purchase QE Invoice

Trx No	Type	Date	Name	Invoice Number	Ref	Details	Net	VAT	Total
19	Purchase QE Invoice	03/07/2016	Radcliff and Sons		Inv 1099		550.00	110.00	660.00
20	Purchase QE Invoice	05/07/2016	Tennison Bros		Inv B-1147		320.00	64.00	384.00
21	Purchase QE Invoice	05/07/2016	Tennison Bros		Inv B-1147		35.00	0.00	35.00
22	Purchase QE Invoice	10/07/2016	Skipton & Co		Inv 2785		938.00	187.60	1,125.60
23	Purchase QE Invoice	10/07/2016	Evelyn Rose		Inv A/5698		671.00	134.20	805.20
						TOTAL	£2,514.00	£495.80	£3,009.80

TASK 11

Customer Activity Report

From: 30/06/2016
To: 31/07/2016

Sports Gear
Customer Activity Report

25 Apr 2017
16:12

J Hollingham (SL01)

Date	Number	Reference	Type	Net	VAT	Total	Discount	Outstanding
30/06/2016		Inv 1001	Customer OB Invoice	3,462.12	0.00	3,462.12		0.00
04/07/2016		Inv 1052	Sales QE Invoice	882.00	176.40	1,058.40		1,058.40
04/07/2016		Inv 1052	Sales QE Invoice	1,023.60	204.72	1,228.32		1,228.32
04/07/2016		Inv 1052	Sales QE Invoice	324.00	64.80	388.80		388.80
17/07/2016		CR34	Sales QE Credit	-510.63	-102.12	-612.75		0.00
19/07/2016		Chq no 542321	Customer Receipt			-2,849.37	0.00	0.00
						2,675.52		2,675.52

Paul McCallum (SL02)

Date	Number	Reference	Type	Net	VAT	Total	Discount	Outstanding
30/06/2016		Inv 0087	Customer OB Invoice	514.68	0.00	514.68		514.68
						514.68		514.68

Kerry Jenkins (SL03)

Date	Number	Reference	Type	Net	VAT	Total	Discount	Outstanding
30/06/2016		Inv 0093	Customer OB Invoice	758.34	0.00	758.34		0.00
06/07/2016		Inv 1053	Sales QE Invoice	132.30	26.46	158.76		158.76
12/07/2016		Chq no 222547	Customer Receipt			-758.34	0.00	0.00
						158.76		158.76

Harry Bucket (SL04)

Date	Number	Reference	Type	Net	VAT	Total	Discount	Outstanding
30/06/2016		Inv 1003	Customer OB Invoice	2,767.34	0.00	2,767.34		0.00
08/07/2016		Inv 1054	Sales QE Invoice	1,513.80	302.76	1,816.56		1,816.56
13/07/2016		BACS	Customer Receipt			-2,767.34	0.00	0.00
						1,816.56		1,816.56

Evelyn Rose (SL05)

Date	Number	Reference	Type	Net	VAT	Total	Discount	Outstanding

From: 30/06/2016
To: 31/07/2016

Sports Gear
Customer Activity Report

25 Apr 2017
16:12

Date	Number	Reference	Type	Net	VAT	Total	Discount	Outstanding
30/06/2016		Inv 1004	Customer OB Invoice	942.98	0.00	942.98		942.98
						942.98		942.98

TASK 11

Supplier Activity Report

Radcliff and Sons (PL01)

Date	Number	Reference	Type	Net	VAT	Total	Discount	Outstanding
30/06/2016		Inv 1874	Supplier OB Invoice	5,362.14	0.00	5,362.14		0.00
03/07/2016		Inv 1099	Purchase QE Invoice	550.00	110.00	660.00		660.00
14/07/2016		Chq no 170012	Supplier Payment			-5,362.14	0.00	0.00
						660.00		660.00

Tennison Bros (PL02)

Date	Number	Reference	Type	Net	VAT	Total	Discount	Outstanding
30/06/2016		Inv B-321	Supplier OB Invoice	2,801.00	0.00	2,801.00		0.00
05/07/2016		Inv B-1147	Purchase QE Invoice	35.00	0.00	35.00		35.00
05/07/2016		Inv B-1147	Purchase QE Invoice	320.00	64.00	384.00		384.00
17/07/2016		Chq no 170013	Supplier Payment			-2,801.00	0.00	0.00
						419.00		419.00

Skipton & Co (PL03)

Date	Number	Reference	Type	Net	VAT	Total	Discount	Outstanding
30/06/2016		Inv 1087	Supplier OB Invoice	501.00	0.00	501.00		501.00
10/07/2016		Inv 2785	Purchase QE Invoice	938.00	187.60	1,125.60		1,125.60
19/07/2016		CX432	Purchase QE Credit	-109.45	-21.89	-131.34		-131.34
						1,495.26		1,495.26

Evelyn Rose (PL04)

Date	Number	Reference	Type	Net	VAT	Total	Discount	Outstanding
30/06/2016		Inv A193	Supplier OB Invoice	250.00	0.00	250.00		250.00
10/07/2016		Inv A/5698	Purchase QE Invoice	671.00	134.20	805.20		805.20
						1,055.20		1,055.20

TASK 11

Aged Creditors Report

| | | | | Sports Gear
Aged Creditors Breakdown | | | | 25 Apr 2017 |
| | | | | | | | | |

| | | To: 31/07/2016 | | | | | | 16:15 |

Date	Reference	Total	Due Date	O/S Amt	< 30 days	< 60 days	< 90 days	Older
Evelyn Rose (PL04), Credit limit: £3,000.00								
, Terms: 30 days - OVERDUE								
10/07/2016	Inv A/5698	805.20	09/08/2016	805.20	805.20			
30/06/2016	Inv A193	250.00	30/07/2016	250.00		250.00		
				£1,055.20	£805.20	£250.00	£0.00	£0.00
Radcliff and Sons (PL01), Credit limit: £15,500.00								
, Terms: 30 days - OVERDUE								
03/07/2016	Inv 1099	660.00	02/08/2016	660.00	660.00			
				£660.00	£660.00	£0.00	£0.00	£0.00
Skipton & Co (PL03), Credit limit: £9,000.00								
, Terms: 30 days - OVERDUE								
19/07/2016	CX432	-131.34		-131.34	-131.34			
30/06/2016	Inv 1087	501.00	30/07/2016	501.00		501.00		
10/07/2016	Inv 2785	1,125.60	09/08/2016	1,125.60	1,125.60			
				£1,495.26	£994.26	£501.00	£0.00	£0.00
Tennison Bros (PL02), Credit limit: £11,000.00								
, Terms: 30 days - OVERDUE								
05/07/2016	Inv B-1147	384.00	04/08/2016	384.00	384.00			
05/07/2016	Inv B-1147	35.00	04/08/2016	35.00	35.00			
				£419.00	£419.00	£0.00	£0.00	£0.00
			TOTAL	£3,629.46	£2,878.46	£751.00	£0.00	£0.00

TASK 11

Aged Debtors Report

| | Sports Gear | | | | | | | 25 Apr 2017 |
| To: 31/07/2016 | Aged Debtors Breakdown | | | | | | | 16:16 |

Date	Reference	Total	Due Date	O/S Amt	< 30 days	< 60 days	< 90 days	Older
Evelyn Rose (SL05), Credit limit: £7,000.00								
, Terms: 30 days - OVERDUE								
30/06/2016	OB-Inv 1004	942.98	30/07/2016	942.98		942.98		
				£942.98	£0.00	£942.98	£0.00	£0.00
Harry Bucket (SL04), Credit limit: £12,000.00								
, Terms: 30 days - OVERDUE								
08/07/2016	QE-Inv 1054	1,816.56	07/08/2016	1,816.56	1,816.56			
				£1,816.56	£1,816.56	£0.00	£0.00	£0.00
J Hollingham (SL01), Credit limit: £5,000.00								
, Terms: 30 days - OVERDUE								
04/07/2016	QE-Inv 1052	1,058.40	03/08/2016	1,058.40	1,058.40			
04/07/2016	QE-Inv 1052	1,228.32	03/08/2016	1,228.32	1,228.32			
04/07/2016	QE-Inv 1052	388.80	03/08/2016	388.80	388.80			
				£2,675.52	£2,675.52	£0.00	£0.00	£0.00
Kerry Jenkins (SL03), Credit limit: £8,000.00								
, Terms: 30 days - OVERDUE								
06/07/2016	QE-Inv 1053	158.76	05/08/2016	158.76	158.76			
				£158.76	£158.76	£0.00	£0.00	£0.00
Paul McCallum (SL02), Credit limit: £9,500.00								
, Terms: 30 days - OVERDUE								
30/06/2016	OB-Inv 0087	514.68	30/07/2016	514.68		514.68		
				£514.68	£0.00	£514.68	£0.00	£0.00
		TOTAL		£6,108.50	£4,650.84	£1,457.66	£0.00	£0.00

TASK 11

Customer Statement

| From: 30/06/2016 | Sports Gear | 25 Apr 2017 |
| To: 31/07/2016 | Statement Summary Report | 16:17 |

Paul McCallum (SL02)
St Albans Road
Seven Kings
Essex
IG7 8DS

Date	Activity	Invoices	Payments	Balance
30/06/2016	Sales Invoice	514.68	0.00	514.68
Summary				
Overdue				514.68

Task 13

Customer change of address

KAPLAN PUBLISHING

TASK 18

TASK 21

Customer Address List

Sports Gear
Customer Address List
27 Apr 2017
10:48

Address Types: All

Customer Name	Address	Contact name	Phone	Mobile	Email	Fax
J Hollingham (SL01)	56 Glencoe Avenue Gants Hill Ilford Essex IG1 6FR	Main Contact				
Paul McCallum (SL02)	St Albans Road Seven Kings Essex IG7 8DS	Main Contact				
Kerry Jenkins (SL03)	34 Gloucester Road Gillingham Kent ME14 3TL	Main Contact				
Harry Bucket (SL04)	137 Chester Road Capel Corner CR3 2SA	Main Contact	08459 754 256			
Evelyn Rose (SL05)	98 Crabtree Drive Bromley Kent DA3 6AY	Main Contact				

TASK 21

Customer Activity (detailed report)

| From: 30/06/2016
To: 31/07/2016 | | | Sports Gear
Customer Activity Report | | | | | 27 Apr 2017
10:50 |

J Hollingham (SL01)

Date	Number	Reference	Type	Net	VAT	Total	Discount	Outstanding
30/06/2016		Inv 1001	Customer OB Invoice	3,462.12	0.00	3,462.12		0.00
04/07/2016		Inv 1052	Sales QE Invoice	882.00	176.40	1,058.40		0.00
04/07/2016		Inv 1052	Sales QE Invoice	1,023.60	204.72	1,228.32		0.00
04/07/2016		Inv 1052	Sales QE Invoice	324.00	64.80	388.80		0.00
17/07/2016		CR34	Sales QE Credit	-510.63	-102.12	-612.75		0.00
19/07/2016		Chq no 542321	Customer Receipt			-2,849.37	0.00	0.00
28/07/2016		Chq no 087651	Customer Receipt			-2,675.52	0.00	0.00
						0.00		0.00

Paul McCallum (SL02)

Date	Number	Reference	Type	Net	VAT	Total	Discount	Outstanding
30/06/2016		Inv 0087	Customer OB Invoice	514.68	0.00	514.68		514.68
						514.68		514.68

Kerry Jenkins (SL03)

Date	Number	Reference	Type	Net	VAT	Total	Discount	Outstanding
30/06/2016		Inv 0093	Customer OB Invoice	758.34	0.00	758.34		0.00
06/07/2016		Inv 1053	Sales QE Invoice	132.30	26.46	158.76		158.76
12/07/2016		Chq no 222547	Customer Receipt			-758.34	0.00	0.00
						158.76		158.76

Harry Bucket (SL04)

Date	Number	Reference	Type	Net	VAT	Total	Discount	Outstanding
30/06/2016		Inv 1003	Customer OB Invoice	2,767.34	0.00	2,767.34		0.00
08/07/2016		Inv 1054	Sales QE Invoice	1,513.80	302.76	1,816.56		1,316.56
13/07/2016		BACS	Customer Receipt			-2,767.34	0.00	0.00
28/07/2016		Chq no 198871	Customer Receipt			-500.00	0.00	0.00
						1,316.56		1,316.56

| From: 30/06/2016
To: 31/07/2016 | | | Sports Gear
Customer Activity Report | | | | | 27 Apr 2017
10:50 |

Evelyn Rose (SL05)

Date	Number	Reference	Type	Net	VAT	Total	Discount	Outstanding
30/06/2016		Inv 1004	Customer OB Invoice	942.98	0.00	942.98		942.98
						942.98		942.98

TASK 21

Supplier Activity (detailed report)

Sports Gear
Supplier Activity Report

Radcliff and Sons (PL01)

Date	Number	Reference	Type	Net	VAT	Total	Discount	Outstanding
30/06/2016		Inv 1874	Supplier OB Invoice	5,362.14	0.00	5,362.14		0.00
03/07/2016		Inv 1099	Purchase QE Invoice	550.00	110.00	660.00		0.00
14/07/2016		Chq no 170012	Supplier Payment			-5,362.14	0.00	0.00
28/07/2016		Chq no 170015	Supplier Payment			-660.00	0.00	0.00
						0.00		0.00

Tennison Bros (PL02)

Date	Number	Reference	Type	Net	VAT	Total	Discount	Outstanding
30/06/2016		Inv B-321	Supplier OB Invoice	2,801.00	0.00	2,801.00		0.00
05/07/2016		Inv B-1147	Purchase QE Invoice	35.00	0.00	35.00		35.00
05/07/2016		Inv B-1147	Purchase QE Invoice	320.00	64.00	384.00		384.00
17/07/2016		Chq no 170013	Supplier Payment			-2,801.00	0.00	0.00
						419.00		419.00

Skipton & Co (PL03)

Date	Number	Reference	Type	Net	VAT	Total	Discount	Outstanding
30/06/2016		Inv 1087	Supplier OB Invoice	501.00	0.00	501.00		0.00
10/07/2016		Inv 2785	Purchase QE Invoice	938.00	187.60	1,125.60		1,125.60
19/07/2016		CX432	Purchase QE Credit	-109.45	-21.89	-131.34		-131.34
28/07/2016		Chq no 170014	Supplier Payment			-501.00	0.00	0.00
						994.26		994.26

Evelyn Rose (PL04)

Date	Number	Reference	Type	Net	VAT	Total	Discount	Outstanding
30/06/2016		Inv A193	Supplier OB Invoice	250.00	0.00	250.00		250.00
10/07/2016		Inv A/5698	Purchase QE Invoice	671.00	134.20	805.20		805.20
						1,055.20		1,055.20

TASK 21

Trial Balance for July

From: 30/06/2016
To: 31/07/2016

Sports Gear
Trial Balance Report

27 Apr 2017
10:56

This period only

Nominal Code	Name	Debit	Credit
0030	Office equipment - Cost	8,430.00	
0040	Fixtures and fittings - Cost	18,000.00	
0050	Motor Vehicles - Cost	15,500.00	
1100	Trade Debtors	2,932.98	
1200	Current	4,924.78	
1210	Cash	300.00	
2100	Trade Creditors		2,468.46
2200	VAT on Sales		5,027.40
2201	VAT on Purchases	1,662.62	
3200	Capital introduced		52,000.00
3260	Drawings - equity	4,735.00	
4000	Sales - Tennis Racquets		16,318.50
4001	Sales - Exercise Bikes		25,222.47
4002	Sales - Golf Clubs		11,101.80
4003	Sales - Fishing Rods		5,968.00
5000	Purchases - Tennis Racquets	21,904.00	
5001	Purchases - Exercise Bikes	25,930.00	
5002	Purchases - Golf Clubs	6,303.55	
5003	Purchases - Fishing Rods	5,467.00	
7200	Electricity	496.06	
7500	Office Stationery	449.90	
7501	Postage	938.55	
7610	Insurance	100.00	
7900	Bank charges and interest	32.19	
	TOTAL	£118,106.63	£118,106.63

TASK 21

Nominal Ledger Activity Report for Bank/Petty Cash

From: 30/06/2016
To: 31/07/2016

Sports Gear
Detailed Nominal Activity: Current (1200)

27 Apr 2017
10:59

Transaction Type: All

Trx No	Date	Invoice Number	Name	Type	Reference	Description	Debit	Credit	Running Total
						Opening Balance		0.00	
10	30/06/2016			Bank Opening Balance			3,325.40		3,325.40 Dr
27	12/07/2016		Kerry Jenkins (SL03)	Customer Receipt	Chq no 222547		758.34		4,083.74 Dr
28	13/07/2016		Harry Bucket (SL04)	Customer Receipt	BACS		2,767.34		6,851.08 Dr
33	13/07/2016			Other Receipt	REC101		1,200.00		8,051.08 Dr
29	14/07/2016		Radcliff and Sons (PL01)	Supplier Payment	Chq no 170012			5,362.14	2,688.94 Dr
41	14/07/2016			Other Receipt	ST5		50.00		2,738.94 Dr
34	15/07/2016			Other Receipt	REC102		2,879.40		5,618.34 Dr
35	15/07/2016			Other Receipt	REC103		1,194.90		6,813.24 Dr
30	17/07/2016		Tennison Bros (PL02)	Supplier Payment	Chq no 170013			2,801.00	4,012.24 Dr
26	19/07/2016		J Hollingham (SL01)	Customer Receipt	Chq no 542321		2,849.37		6,861.61 Dr
42	19/07/2016			Other Receipt	Debit card		54.00		6,915.61 Dr
36	25/07/2016			Journal	JNL004			3,441.00	3,474.61 Dr
37	28/07/2016		Skipton & Co (PL03)	Supplier Payment	Chq no 170014			501.00	2,973.61 Dr
38	28/07/2016		Radcliff and Sons (PL01)	Supplier Payment	Chq no 170015			660.00	2,313.61 Dr
39	28/07/2016		J Hollingham (SL01)	Customer Receipt	Chq no 087651		2,675.52		4,989.13 Dr
40	28/07/2016		Harry Bucket (SL04)	Customer Receipt	Chq no 198871		500.00		5,489.13 Dr
44	28/07/2016			Other Payment	Ipswich Union - SO			100.00	5,389.13 Dr
53	31/07/2016			Bank Payment	Bank Charge			32.19	5,356.94 Dr
54	31/07/2016			Bank Transfer	TRF01			432.16	4,924.78 Dr
						Closing Balance	4,924.78		
						Period Variance	4,924.78		

From: 30/06/2016
To: 31/07/2016

Sports Gear
Detailed Nominal Activity: Cash (1210)

27 Apr 2017
11:01

Transaction Type: All

Trx No	Date	Invoice Number	Name	Type	Reference	Description	Debit	Credit	Running Total
						Opening Balance		0.00	
11	30/06/2016			Bank Opening Balance			300.00		300.00 Dr
31	10/07/2016			Other Payment	Voucher no 152			19.90	280.10 Dr
32	20/07/2016			Other Payment	Voucher no 187			412.26	132.16 Cr
54	31/07/2016			Bank Transfer	TRF01		432.16		300.00 Dr
						Closing Balance	300.00		
						Period Variance	300.00		

PRACTICE PAPER 5

WAY TO WORK ANSWERS

TASK 3.3

Customer Address List

	Way To Work Customer Address List						11 May 2017 14:14

Address Types: All

Customer Name	Address	Contact name	Phone	Mobile	Email	Fax
Morgan, Smith & Winston (JP01)	City Road Islington London N1 9PL	Main Contact				
Cyril West (JP02)	Grays West Grays Inn Road London WC1 1LT	Main Contact				
Wallace & Gromit Ltd (JP03)	134 Upper Street Islington London N1 2PT	Main Contact				
Star Paper (JP04)	66 White Lion Street London N1 5RX	Main Contact				

TASK 3.3

Supplier Address List

	Way To Work Supplier Address List						11 May 2017 14:21

Address Types: All

Supplier Name	Address	Contact name	Phone	Mobile	Email	Fax
Paper Products UK (SP01)	South Down Trading Estate Sheffield S15 4DR	Main Contact				
Wallace & Gromit Ltd (SP02)	134 Upper Street Islington London N1 2PT	Main Contact				
Whole Office Furniture (SP03)	176 East Way Leeds LD4 6PP	Main Contact				
Stationery World (SP04)	32 Great Portland Road London WC1V 6HH	Main Contact				

TASK 3.3

Trial Balance

| From: 29/02/2016 | Way To Work | 11 May 2017 |
| To: 31/03/2016 | **Trial Balance Report** | 14:23 |

This period only

Nominal Code	Name	Selected Period	
		Debit	Credit
0040	Fixtures and fittings - Cost	8,000.00	
0050	Motor Vehicles - Cost	14,000.00	
1100	Trade Debtors	9,173.68	
1200	Current	4,710.81	
1210	Cash	100.00	
1220	Deposit	1,500.00	
2100	Trade Creditors		18,535.76
3200	Capital introduced		34,000.00
3260	Drawings - equity	1,000.00	
4000	Stationery Sales		903.73
4001	CD Rom Sales		855.00
4002	Printer Accessories Sales		9,842.00
5000	Stationery Purchases	2,400.00	
5001	CD Rom Purchases	210.00	
5002	Printer Accessory Purchases	15,000.00	
7000	Wages and Salaries	5,600.00	
7100	Rent and rates	2,100.00	
8200	General Expenses	342.00	
	TOTAL	**£64,136.49**	**£64,136.49**

TASK 9

Remittance Advice

Date Paid: 31/03/2016

Reference: SP01

Paper Products UK South Down Trading Estate Sheffield S15 4DR	**Way To Work** 55 Upper Street London N1 9PE United Kingdom Telephone: 01234 567891 VAT Number: GB 123456789

Reference: Chq no 100076

Our Ref	Your Ref	Date	Total Amount	Amount Paid
Inv 0165		29/02/2016	445.23	445.23
		Total Paid:		**£ 445.23 GBP**

Task 9

Remittance Advice

Date Paid: 31/03/2016

Reference: SP03

Whole Office Furniture 176 East Way Leeds LD4 6PP	**Way To Work** 55 Upper Street London N1 9PE United Kingdom Telephone: 01234 567891 VAT Number: GB 123456789

Reference: Chq no 100077

Our Ref	Your Ref	Date	Total Amount	Amount Paid
Inv 1028		29/02/2016	1,875.21	1,875.21
		Total Paid:		**£ 1,875.21 GBP**

Task 9

Remittance Advice

Date Paid: 31/03/2016

Reference: SP04

Stationery World 32 Great Portland Road London WC1V 6HH	**Way To Work** 55 Upper Street London N1 9PE United Kingdom Telephone: 01234 567891 VAT Number: GB 123456789

Reference: Chq no 100078

Our Ref	Your Ref	Date	Total Amount	Amount Paid
Inv 0187		29/02/2016	9,504.32	9,504.32
			Total Paid:	**£ 9,504.32 GBP**

TASK 13

Recurring payment

TASK 15

Customer Activity (detailed report)

From: 29/02/2016
To: 31/03/2016

Way To Work
Customer Activity Report

11 May 2017
15:38

Morgan, Smith & Winston (JP01)

Date	Number	Reference	Type	Net	VAT	Total	Discount	Outstanding
29/02/2016		INV021	Customer OB Invoice	1,172.34	0.00	1,172.34		0.00
05/03/2016		INV043	Sales QE Invoice	4,376.00	875.20	5,251.20		5,251.20
07/03/2016		INV45	Sales QE Invoice	6,210.00	1,242.00	7,452.00		7,452.00
15/03/2016		Chqno 203998	Customer Receipt			-1,172.34	0.00	0.00
						12,703.20		12,703.20

Cyril West (JP02)

Date	Number	Reference	Type	Net	VAT	Total	Discount	Outstanding
29/02/2016		INV045	Customer OB Invoice	2,954.00	0.00	2,954.00		0.00
03/03/2016		INV041	Sales QE Invoice	780.00	156.00	936.00		936.00
17/03/2016		Chq no 103112	Customer Receipt			-2,954.00	0.00	0.00
						936.00		936.00

Wallace & Gromit Ltd (JP03)

Date	Number	Reference	Type	Net	VAT	Total	Discount	Outstanding
29/02/2016		INV033	Customer OB Invoice	3,180.00	0.00	3,180.00		3,180.00
07/03/2016		INV044	Sales QE Invoice	458.00	91.60	549.60		549.60
						3,729.60		3,729.60

Star Paper (JP04)

Date	Number	Reference	Type	Net	VAT	Total	Discount	Outstanding
29/02/2016		INV034	Customer OB Invoice	1,867.34	0.00	1,867.34		0.00
03/03/2016		INV042	Sales QE Invoice	921.00	184.20	1,105.20		1,105.20
17/03/2016		CR51	Sales QE Credit	-251.27	-50.25	-301.52		0.00
19/03/2016		Chq no 011211	Customer Receipt			-1,565.82	0.00	0.00
						1,105.20		1,105.20

TASK 15

Supplier Activity (detailed report)

From: 29/02/2016
To: 31/03/2016

Way To Work
Supplier Activity Report

11 May 2017
15:42

Paper Products UK (SP01)

Date	Number	Reference	Type	Net	VAT	Total	Discount	Outstanding
29/02/2016		Inv 0165	Supplier OB Invoice	445.23	0.00	445.23		0.00
10/03/2016		0200	Purchase QE Invoice	489.00	97.80	586.80		586.80
31/03/2016		Chq no 100076	Supplier Payment			-445.23	0.00	0.00
						586.80		586.80

Wallace & Gromit Ltd (SP02)

Date	Number	Reference	Type	Net	VAT	Total	Discount	Outstanding
29/02/2016		Inv 02183	Supplier OB Invoice	6,711.00	0.00	6,711.00		6,711.00
11/03/2016		02241	Purchase QE Invoice	345.00	69.00	414.00		414.00
						7,125.00		7,125.00

Whole Office Furniture (SP03)

Date	Number	Reference	Type	Net	VAT	Total	Discount	Outstanding
29/02/2016		Inv 1028	Supplier OB Invoice	1,875.21	0.00	1,875.21		0.00
11/03/2016		1098	Purchase QE Invoice	7,628.00	1,525.60	9,153.60		9,153.60
31/03/2016		Chq no 100077	Supplier Payment			-1,875.21	0.00	0.00
						9,153.60		9,153.60

Stationery World (SP04)

Date	Number	Reference	Type	Net	VAT	Total	Discount	Outstanding
29/02/2016		Inv 0187	Supplier OB Invoice	9,504.32	0.00	9,504.32		0.00
14/03/2016		0197	Purchase QE Invoice	3,567.00	713.40	4,280.40		4,280.40
19/03/2016		RF287	Purchase QE Credit	-124.08	-24.82	-148.90		-148.90
31/03/2016		Chq no 100078	Supplier Payment			-9,504.32	0.00	0.00
						4,131.50		4,131.50

TASK 15

Trial Balance

From: 29/02/2016	Way To Work	12 May 2017
To: 31/03/2016	**Trial Balance Report**	11:13

This period only

Nominal Code	Name	Debit	Credit
0040	Fixtures and fittings - Cost	8,000.00	
0050	Motor Vehicles - Cost	14,000.00	
1100	Trade Debtors	18,474.00	
1200	Current		2,589.76
1210	Petty Cash	206.68	
1220	Deposit	1,500.00	
2100	Trade Creditors		20,996.90
2200	VAT on Sales		2,519.33
2201	VAT on Purchases	2,463.20	
3200	Capital introduced		34,000.00
3260	Drawings - equity	1,000.00	
4000	Stationery Sales		7,893.73
4001	CD Rom Sales		1,776.00
4002	Printer Accessories Sales		14,527.63
5000	Stationery Purchases	6,331.92	
5001	CD Rom Purchases	555.00	
5002	Printer Accessory Purchases	22,628.00	
6201	Advertising	327.00	
7000	Wages and Salaries	5,600.00	
7100	Rent and rates	2,668.00	
7200	Gas and electric	84.10	
7900	Bank charges and interest	123.45	
8200	General Expenses	342.00	
	TOTAL	**£84,303.35**	**£84,303.35**

TASK 15

Audit Trail for March (inc opening balances)

From: 29/02/2016
To: 31/03/2016

Way To Work
Audit Trail Breakdown

12 May 2017
11:16

Type: All, Status: All

Trx No	Entry Date	User	Trx Date	Name	Type	Invoice Number	Ref	Ledger Account	Debit	Credit	Bank Reconciled
1	11/05/2017	LH	29/02/2016	Morgan, Smith & Winston (JP01)	Customer OB Invoice		INV021	Opening Balances Control Account (9998)		1,172.34	No
								Trade Debtors (1100)	1,172.34		No
2	11/05/2017	LH	29/02/2016	Cyril West (JP02)	Customer OB Invoice		INV045	Opening Balances Control Account (9998)		2,954.00	No
								Trade Debtors (1100)	2,954.00		No
3	11/05/2017	LH	29/02/2016	Wallsce & Gromit Ltd (JP03)	Customer OB Invoice		INV033	Opening Balances Control Account (9998)		3,180.00	No
								Trade Debtors (1100)	3,180.00		No
4	11/05/2017	LH	29/02/2016	Star Paper (JP04)	Customer OB Invoice		INV034	Opening Balances Control Account (9998)		1,867.34	No
								Trade Debtors (1100)	1,867.34		No
5	11/05/2017	LH	29/02/2016	Paper Products UK (SP01)	Supplier OB Invoice		Inv 0165	Trade Creditors (2100)		445.23	No
								Opening Balances Control Account (9998)	445.23		No
6	11/05/2017	LH	29/02/2016	Wallsce & Gromit Ltd (SP02)	Supplier OB Invoice		Inv 02183	Trade Creditors (2100)		6,711.00	No
								Opening Balances Control Account (9998)	6,711.00		No
7	11/05/2017	LH	29/02/2016	Whole Office Furniture (SP03)	Supplier OB Invoice		Inv 1028	Trade Creditors (2100)		1,875.21	No
								Opening Balances Control Account (9998)	1,875.21		No
8	11/05/2017	LH	29/02/2016	Stationery World (SP04)	Supplier OB Invoice		Inv 0187	Trade Creditors (2100)		9,504.32	No
								Opening Balances Control Account (9998)	9,504.32		No
9	11/05/2017	LH	29/02/2016		Bank Opening Balance			Opening Balances Control Account (9998)		6,210.81	No
								Current (1200)	6,210.81		Yes
10	11/05/2017	LH	29/02/2016		Bank Opening Balance			Opening Balances Control Account (9998)		100.00	No
								Petty Cash (1210)	100.00		No
11	11/05/2017	LH	29/02/2016		Journal Opening Balance		OB 1/3/16	Motor Vehicles - Cost (0050)	14,000.00		No
								Opening Balances Control Account (9998)		14,000.00	No

Produced by Sage One

From: 29/02/2016
To: 31/03/2016

Way To Work
Audit Trail Breakdown

12 May 2017
11:16

Trx No	Entry Date	User	Trx Date	Name	Type	Invoice Number	Ref	Ledger Account	Debit	Credit	Bank Reconciled
								Fixtures and fittings - Cost (0040)	8,000.00		No
								Opening Balances Control Account (9998)		8,000.00	No
								Capital introduced (3200)		34,000.00	No
								Opening Balances Control Account (9998)	34,000.00		No
								Drawings - equity (3260)	1,000.00		No
								Opening Balances Control Account (9998)		1,000.00	No
								Stationery Sales (4000)		903.73	No
								Opening Balances Control Account (9998)	903.73		No
								CD Rom Sales (4001)		855.00	No
								Opening Balances Control Account (9998)	855.00		No
								Printer Accessories Sales (4002)		9,842.00	No
								Opening Balances Control Account (9998)	9,842.00		No
								Stationery Purchases (5000)	2,400.00		No
								Opening Balances Control Account (9998)		2,400.00	No
								CD Rom Purchases (5001)	210.00		No
								Opening Balances Control Account (9998)		210.00	No
								Printer Accessory Purchases (5002)	15,000.00		No
								Opening Balances Control Account (9998)		15,000.00	No
								Wages and Salaries (7000)	5,600.00		No
								Opening Balances Control Account (9998)		5,600.00	No
								General Expenses (8200)	342.00		No
								Opening Balances Control Account (9998)		342.00	No
								Rent and rates (7100)	2,100.00		No
								Opening Balances Control Account (9998)		2,100.00	No
12	11/05/2017	LH	01/03/2016		Bank Transfer		TRANS01	Current (1200)		1,500.00	Yes
								Deposit (1220)	1,500.00		No

Produced by Sage One

133

From: 29/02/2016
To: 31/03/2016

Way To Work
Audit Trail Breakdown

12 May 2017
11:16

No	Date		Date	Name	Type	Ref	Account	Debit	Credit	Bank
13	11/05/2017	LH	03/03/2016	Cyril West (JP02)	Sales QE Invoice	INV041	Stationery Sales (4000)		780.00	No
							VAT on Sales (2200)		156.00	No
							Trade Debtors (1100)	936.00		No
14	11/05/2017	LH	03/03/2016	Star Paper (JP04)	Sales QE Invoice	INV042	CD Rom Sales (4001)		921.00	No
							VAT on Sales (2200)		184.20	No
							Trade Debtors (1100)	1,105.20		No
15	11/05/2017	LH	05/03/2016	Morgan, Smith & Winston (JP01)	Sales QE Invoice	INV043	Printer Accessories Sales (4002)		4,376.00	No
							VAT on Sales (2200)		875.20	No
							Trade Debtors (1100)	5,251.20		No
16	11/05/2017	LH	07/03/2016	Wallace & Gromit Ltd (JP03)	Sales QE Invoice	INV044	Printer Accessories Sales (4002)		458.00	No
							VAT on Sales (2200)		91.60	No
							Trade Debtors (1100)	549.60		No
17	11/05/2017	LH	07/03/2016	Morgan, Smith & Winston (JP01)	Sales QE Invoice	INV45	Stationery Sales (4000)		6,210.00	No
							VAT on Sales (2200)		1,242.00	No
							Trade Debtors (1100)	7,452.00		No
18	11/05/2017	LH	17/03/2016	Star Paper (JP04)	Sales QE Credit	CR51	Trade Debtors (1100)		301.52	No
							Printer Accessories Sales (4002)	251.27		No
							VAT on Sales (2200)	50.25		No
19	11/05/2017	LH	10/03/2016	Paper Products UK (SP01)	Purchase QE Invoice	0200	Trade Creditors (2100)		586.80	No
							Stationery Purchases (5000)	489.00		No
							VAT on Purchases (2201)	97.80		No
20	11/05/2017	LH	11/03/2016	Wallace & Gromit Ltd (SP02)	Purchase QE Invoice	02241	Trade Creditors (2100)		414.00	No
							CD Rom Purchases (5001)	345.00		No
							VAT on Purchases (2201)	69.00		No
21	11/05/2017	LH	11/03/2016	Whole Office Furniture (SP03)	Purchase QE Invoice	1096	Trade Creditors (2100)		9,153.60	No
							Printer Accessory Purchases (5002)	7,628.00		No

From: 29/02/2016
To: 31/03/2016

Way To Work
Audit Trail Breakdown

12 May 2017
11:16

No	Date		Date	Name	Type	Ref	Account	Debit	Credit	Bank
							VAT on Purchases (2201)	1,525.60		No
22	11/05/2017	LH	14/03/2016	Stationery World (SP04)	Purchase QE Invoice	0197	Trade Creditors (2100)		4,280.40	No
							Stationery Purchases (5000)	3,567.00		No
							VAT on Purchases (2201)	713.40		No
23	11/05/2017	LH	19/03/2016	Stationery World (SP04)	Purchase QE Credit	RF287	Stationery Purchases (5000)		124.06	No
							VAT on Purchases (2201)		24.82	No
							Trade Creditors (2100)	148.90		No
24	11/05/2017	LH	15/03/2016	Morgan, Smith & Winston (JP01)	Customer Receipt	Chqno 203998	Trade Debtors (1100)		1,172.34	No
							Current (1200)	1,172.34		Yes
25	11/05/2017	LH	17/03/2016	Cyril West (JP02)	Customer Receipt	Chq no 103112	Trade Debtors (1100)		2,954.00	No
							Current (1200)	2,954.00		Yes
26	11/05/2017	LH	19/03/2016	Star Paper (JP04)	Customer Receipt	Chq no 011211	Trade Debtors (1100)		1,867.34	No
							Trade Debtors (1100)	301.52		No
							Current (1200)	1,565.82		Yes
27	11/05/2017	LH	31/03/2016	Paper Products UK (SP01)	Supplier Payment	Chq no 100076	Trade Creditors (2100)	445.23		No
							Current (1200)		445.23	Yes
28	11/05/2017	LH	31/03/2016	Whole Office Furniture (SP03)	Supplier Payment	Chq no 100077	Trade Creditors (2100)	1,875.21		No
							Current (1200)		1,875.21	Yes
29	11/05/2017	LH	31/03/2016	Stationery World (SP04)	Supplier Payment	Chq no 100078	Trade Creditors (2100)	9,504.32		No
							Current (1200)		9,504.32	No
30	11/05/2017	LH	15/03/2016		Bank Transfer	TRANS02	Current (1200)		600.00	Yes
							Petty Cash (1210)	600.00		No
31	11/05/2017	LH	19/03/2016		Other Payment	Petty cash voucher 056	Petty Cash (1210)		100.92	No
							Gas and electric (7200)	96.11		No
							VAT on Purchases (2201)	4.81		No
							Petty Cash (1210)	100.92		No

From: 29/02/2016
To: 31/03/2016

Way To Work
Audit Trail Breakdown

12 May 2017
11:16

						Gas and electric (7200)	96.11	No
						VAT on Purchases (2201)	4.81	No
32	11/05/2017	LH	19/03/2016	Other Payment	Petty cash voucher 056	Petty Cash (1210)	100.92	No
						Gas and electric (7200)	84.10	No
						VAT on Purchases (2201)	16.82	No
33	11/05/2017	LH	20/03/2016	Other Payment	Petty cash voucher 057	Petty Cash (1210)	392.40	No
						Advertising (6201)	327.00	No
						VAT on Purchases (2201)	65.40	No
34	11/05/2017	LH	26/03/2016	Other Receipt	ST4	Printer Accessories Sales (4002)	102.90	No
						VAT on Sales (2200)	20.58	No
						Current (1200)	123.48	Yes
36	11/05/2017	LH	31/03/2016	Other Payment	standing order rent	Current (1200)	568.00	Yes
						Rent and rates (7100)	568.00	No
						VAT on Purchases (2201)		No
48	11/05/2017	LH	31/03/2016	Bank Payment	Bank Charge	Current (1200)	123.45	Yes
						Bank charges and interest (7900)	123.45	No

TASK 15

Nominal Ledger Activity for Bank/Petty Cash

From: 29/02/2016
To: 31/03/2016

Way To Work
Detailed Nominal Activity ent (1200)

12 May 2017
11:07

Transaction Type: All

Trx No	Date	Invoice Number	Name	Type	Reference	Description	Debit	Credit	Running Total
						Opening Balance		0.00	
9	29/02/2016			Bank Opening Balance			6,210.81		6,210.81 Dr
12	01/03/2016			Bank Transfer	TRANS01			1,500.00	4,710.81 Dr
24	15/03/2016		Morgan, Smith & Winston (JP01)	Customer Receipt	Chqno 203998		1,172.34		5,883.15 Dr
30	15/03/2016			Bank Transfer	TRANS02			600.00	5,283.15 Dr
25	17/03/2016		Cyril West (JP02)	Customer Receipt	Chq no 103112		2,954.00		8,237.15 Dr
26	19/03/2016		Star Paper (JP04)	Customer Receipt	Chq no 011211		1,565.82		9,802.97 Dr
34	26/03/2016			Other Receipt	ST4		123.48		9,926.45 Dr
27	31/03/2016		Paper Products UK (SP01)	Supplier Payment	Chq no 100076			445.23	9,481.22 Dr
28	31/03/2016		Whole Office Furniture (SP03)	Supplier Payment	Chq no 100077			1,875.21	7,606.01 Dr
29	31/03/2016		Stationery World (SP04)	Supplier Payment	Chq no 100078			9,504.32	1,898.31 Cr
36	31/03/2016			Other Payment	standing order rent			568.00	2,466.31 Cr
48	31/03/2016			Bank Payment	Bank Charge			123.45	2,589.76 Cr
						Closing Balance	2,589.76		
						Period Variance	2,589.76		

From: 29/02/2016
To: 31/03/2016

Way To Work
Detailed Nominal Activity: Petty Cash (1210)

12 May 2017
11:24

Transaction Type: All

Trx No	Date	Invoice Number	Name	Type	Reference	Description	Debit	Credit	Running Total
						Opening Balance		0.00	
10	29/02/2016			Bank Opening Balance			100.00		100.00 Dr
30	15/03/2016			Bank Transfer	TRANS02		600.00		700.00 Dr
32	19/03/2016			Other Payment	Petty cash voucher 056			100.92	599.08 Dr
33	20/03/2016			Other Payment	Petty cash voucher 057			392.40	206.68 Dr
						Closing Balance	206.68		
						Period Variance	206.68